What Ea

"These pieces reflect deep compassion and committed empathy. I read it in one sitting." – Maggie D.

"The way it is written is just beautiful. The book is full of emotion, and one can feel that it's sprouting directly from the heart." – Satdeep G.

"Fantastically raw." – Gabe O.

"I was laughing and crying. The book is educating me on many levels." - Susan O.

"The writing has an intelligence, a vulnerability, and the most perfect use of English vocabulary. What all of it has in common is an openness, an honesty, a kindness, and an ability to grab the reader. The style is so refreshing and unusual, especially in today's world." – Kathy G.

"It moved me." – Sue C.

"I loved the blend of loving didactic, poetic expression, and suspense novel style of the book." – Dee S.

I dedicate this book to the psychiatrist, whose name I can no longer recall, who told me in that locked room, "It's not too late to have everything you want, but one day it will be."

To my mom, who pulled the trigger when no one else would to slay my demons.

To my dad, who wouldn't ever not defend me.

To my sisters, who went before me and charted a path home.

To my friends, who came back again and again.

To my wife, who was worth returning to the world for.

To all those who have suffered or are suffering.

To the pursuit of life at its fullest.

To hope.

Welcome

Hi, my name is Jake Orlowitz and I wrote this book, *Welcome to the Circle*. I wrote it to tell my story, and I wrote it for you.

Mental health isn't easy to talk about, so I wrote this book to help people on their personal journeys of illness and recovery. I wrote it for people whose loved ones are struggling, who they are trying to help but don't know how to help. I also wrote it to deepen compassion and acceptance across society. Mental illness can interrupt lives—but doesn't have to be their defining tragedy.

I never expected to wind up in a mental hospital. I was class treasurer in my student council, elected to our ceremonial homecoming court, varsity wrestling champion, head of my academic class, and a distinguished college graduate. But life threw me an unexpected turn. After college my mental health suddenly declined. Anxiety turned into phobia. Depression into despair. Frustration into rage. Irritability into wild mood swings. I went from being a happy, social person, full of life and humor, to someone who desperately wanted to avoid the world and couldn't tolerate its onslaught of stimulation and slights.

Mental illness is not a dead end, however. It can be a powerful beginning. In the seven years since I was hospitalized, I found effective treatment with both therapy and medications. I reconnected with family and made friends from around the world. I started a successful global initiative for Wikipedia. I met and married my strong, brilliant, beautiful wife. I became a stepfather to her incredible daughter. Along the way, I also learned and practiced how to help others find their own way into recovery.

This book is my story and the multitude of lessons I've learned along the way. More than just memoir, the book is a meditation on the mental health journeys all of us must take to become better humans. It is full of useful advice about how to navigate mental illness in all its difficulty and unpredictability, either for you, or for the ones you love.

In 28 different pieces, I cover mental illness and loss—the hard parts—as well as redemption and gratitude—the hopeful aspects. The focus can be intimately personal at times, broadly applicable to treatment in general, or boldly exploring society at large. Dive into the essays, sit down with the poems, tick through the lists, and dig into the guides. I truly hope they add insight, understanding, empathy, and practical knowledge to your life.

I want to invite you into the conversation I've been having, for the last seven years, about mental illness and mental health, recovery and redemption, life and loss, healing and hope.

Welcome to the Circle. Thank you for being here.

Contents

Journey of a Wikipedian	8
Horizon	12
A Few Thoughts for Being in a Movement	14
OK COMPUTER	15
True Stories Aren't Always Easy to Tell	16
Liminal	27
Sex and Sanity	29
Welcome to the Circle	31
How to Save Someone's Life (Part 1)	34
Convenience	39
A Eulogy for Paradon	41
If I Can Make It	46
Stonefruit	49
How to Save Someone's Life (Part 2)	51
The Atomic Method	57
Haikus	60
Curated Thoughts for Inadvertent Witnesses	68
The Crisis Killing Our Boys	70
Before Sean	76
How to Save Someone's Life (Part 3)	80
Hamsa	94

How to Write a Facebook Suicide Note	**95**
What Do We Do Now?	**97**
How to Save Someone's Life (Part 4)	**98**
Humans of Planet Earth	**100**
Sedona	**102**
I Am Feeling Lucky Now	**103**
Hafiz Remixed on the Eve of My Wedding	**109**
For Those Seeking Support	**110**
Parting Thoughts	**112**
Acknowledgements	**113**
About the Author	**115**

Choose Your Own Adventures

Essays
Journey of a Wikipedian, True Stories Aren't Always Easy to Tell, Sex and Sanity, A Eulogy for Paradon, The Crisis Killing Our Boys, Humans of Planet Earth, I Am Feeling Lucky Now

Poems
Horizon, OK COMPUTER, Liminal, Convenience, Stonefruit, Haikus, Before Sean, Hamsa, How to Save Someone's Life (Part 4), Sedona, Hafiz Remixed on the Eve of My Wedding

Lists
A Few Thoughts for Being in a Movement, Welcome to the Circle, If I Can Make It, Curated Thoughts for Inadvertent Witnesses, How to Write a Facebook Suicide Note

Guides
How to Save Someone's Life (Part 1), How to Save Someone's Life (Part 2), The Atomic Method, How to Save Someone's Life (Part 3), What Do We Do Now?

"Hope is a verb with its sleeves rolled up."

– David Orr, Philosopher

"You're playing it too close to the vest."

– Jim, My Wrestling Coach

"Honey, you're a genius!"

– Sally, My Grandmother

"God damn it, you've got to be kind."

– Kurt Vonnegut, Writer

"I love you, but you're cray."

– Siko, My Wife

Journey of a Wikipedian

There's no one moment when you go insane;
not when
you find yourself crying into a phone behind a closet door
or tapping your foot to neutralize thoughts you can't handle
or sleeping on a bed of worn clothes on a hard floor
or when the police officer pulls you over again for driving
up and back the same stretch of highway, six times
and not when you physically *crack* the monitor in a dark room
for no reason even though it was the only light left in a night's
center as you tap away at keys throughout the silence

But you occasionally get a glimpse of someone else realizing that "you've lost it".

It was probably fall 2010. My dad turned the knob on the attic bathroom door in the house where I had grown up, and the reaction on his face was devastated. He didn't know that no other room in the house, or the country, felt safe to me, that the warm water soothed and wetted the dry, frigid air, that my laptop was balanced purposefully so that it would fall backwards onto the tile rather than into the hip-high water, and that I had chosen the high ledge of the tub for its ergonomic watchlist-monitoring suitability.

He didn't know that. He just saw his 27-year-old son, feverishly tinkering with electronics on the edge of a full bath, completely nude, oblivious to anything else, or anything wrong. He also didn't know that I was helping lead the Egyptian revolution.

That too sounds insane, but as the calendar flipped into January 2011, the new year brought millions to Egypt's streets. A boy had gone missing, turned up in a morgue clearly beaten beyond breath by police. Facebook pages organized gatherings that filled immense public squares. Protests turned into uprising turned into revolution.

And I, alongside four exceptionally dedicated editors from three different continents, monitored the 2011 Egyptian Revolution Wikipedia article 24-hours-a-day with balance and fervor. We yearned for Mubarak to fall, but in the newsroom which the article's talkpage had become, we were vigilantly checking multiple independent reports before inputting any new words onto the growing page, scouring the article for flourishes of revolutionary support. The world would come here to find the facts—those that would dispassionately drive understanding without embellishment or bias for the hundreds of thousands of people reading that page each day. And I would make sure of it. From my bathtub.

There's also no one time when sanity returns, if there is such a defined state. But suffice to say that it builds upon moments.

Like the moment when you start talking off-channel to a Wikipedian on Internet Relay Chat, just to speak to someone again. Or when you put on a suit for the first time in six years, to give a talk on conflict-of-interest to a gathering of PR pros at a posh downtown bar. Or when you step into the hostel at Wikimania in 2012 in D.C. and meet robot anthropologist Stu Geiger, your coincidental bunkmate, and instantly recognize his familiar, Wikipedian-ite, eclectic genius.

The moments gather momentum though. Soon you are calling up major publishing companies to ask for donations. Not as Jake, or that guy who lost a decade in his 20s, or the model teenager who lapsed into dysfunction and veered "off course". But calling rather, as a piece-of-Wikipedia... Do you know what doors that opens?

The drama of recovery shouldn't be overly simplified into highlights. It was just as much my psychiatrist's expert balancing—seeking of psychic neutrality—with a fine and formidable mix of anxiolytics, antidepressants, antipsychotics, and sleep aids. Not too high, not too low. Not too moody, not too flat. Every pill presented a trade-off, but we found a consensus pharmacology that worked.

My parents made sure that my rock bottom was somewhere safe.

My friends' surprise visits reminded me that there was fun yet to be had.

The diagnoses I received were varied and all increasingly off-the mark. I was bipolar, but generally calm through even the grittiest edit wars. I was agoraphobic and socially anxious, but traveling to Hong Kong and Quebec and Berlin for meetups with strangers from myriad countries. I was depressed, but could not control an urge to improve a bit of Wikipedia, every day, most of the day.

They say that Wikipedia is "Not Therapy". It's a serious place to write an encyclopedia, not to iron out one's mental kinks or cracks. But I think that's wrong. No one knew me on Wikipedia, except for my words, the wisdom of my input, and the value of my contributions. They couldn't care less if I was manic, phobic, delusional, or hysterical. It just didn't matter. They didn't see that part of me.

So I got to build my identity, my confidence, my vocation—with long-winded eloquent analyses, meticulous bibliographies, and copious rewrites of difficult subjects.

They also say that wikipedia is "Not A Social Network", but that's wrong too. In the eight years since I started editing, first in my car outside a Starbucks, and then throughout the dull shifts of a mountain-town Staples store where I squatted for Wi-Fi, and then still more through three years back at home under blankets between dusk and dawn, I met hundreds of people with whom I shared the same passion. I received, quite marvelously, 49 barnstars from peers, friends, and fans. There wasn't a bigger or better sense of validation.

I received two incomparable partners, to build a Wikipedia Library that I created and had become the head of. I received a job offer, with wellness benefits. I also received, in the grand sense of things, an irrepressible, stunning, and brilliant girlfriend and her exuberant five-year-old daughter into my life.

You see, Wikipedia brings people together. It brought me together. It just takes some time for everyone to get their heads on straight, before they can see that their lives too have a mission, and an [edit] button.

Horizon

I sat by the abyss one afternoon
Dangling my legs over the edge

It was quiet there
And surprisingly warm
Like the flush one gets from hypothermia
Or the accretion disk of a black hole

A friend was kind enough
To join me
And he listened
He didn't dangle his legs
That would have been too much
But he was comfortable all the same

We sat for a while
I told him what I saw
Staring into the void
Then he put his hand softly on my back
And told me it was time for him to go

The abyss is
A nice place to visit
Maybe for a day
Set up a chair on the cliff of darkness
Watch the weary pieces of the world
Fall in

My friend joined me on the edge one afternoon
And he listened
I had no idea how many times
I would have to return the favor
When I went back I sat

With legs crossed
I was wiser
And he was in danger
And despite all my love
We were both terrified

You can be a hero without speaking a word
Tie your ropes
Tell someone where you've gone
And head back by sunset

Even with good company
The abyss is
No place to spend the night

A Few Thoughts for Being in a Movement

1. We are a mix of very real people with deep emotions and human complexities.

2. We are deeply invested in our projects, so much it hurts us at times, even if they are also a passion or a refuge.

3. You never know what someone has been through, or is going through.

4. We all need help at some point. There is no shame in needing help, asking for help, or receiving help.

5. If you are ever feeling completely hopeless: Wait. Things really can get better. Talk to someone about it.

6. If we listen, we can learn from each other.

7. We need to be kind. This is a higher calling than civility, and entirely compatible with achieving our goals.

8. Our community depends on its people. We are our most valuable resource.

9. We are not finished products. With time, space, support, and practice—people can, and do, grow and change.

OK COMPUTER

I made myself so extra small
the screen my only sun
to fit between the sunken wires
until the night was done

I made myself so extra small
to float up to the cloud
not single a soul could see me
my username my shroud

I made myself so extra small
and wandered through the tubes
my identity in pieces
all broken into cubes

I made myself so extra small
composed of ones and zeroes
the lag my only enemy
the download speeds my heroes

I made myself so extra small
to flit from node to node
you really cannot get too lost
when the internet's your road

I made myself so extra small
there were no bits to save
when you're living in computers
there's no need to be brave

I made myself so extra small
my secrets only passwords
with "hello, world" my starting phrase
and "power off" my last words

True Stories Aren't Always Easy to Tell

"Are you travelling alone?" the flight attendant asked with a polite urgency. I was one row from the very back of the plane, but had settled into an aisle seat where I could at least recline, stretch out my leg, and not have to hop over people to reach the restroom. I like to hydrate when I travel. It gets stuffy on an airplane.

A brown-skinned man walked towards us, plaintive and looking like he was missing something. "This man would like to sit closer to his wife and two children in the row behind you," the attendant said. I paused, thinking of karma and good deeds. "There's a middle seat waiting for you all the way up front in row 11."

"You'll get off sooner," she suggests with a half-sincere smile.

"I'd be happy to."

I grabbed my backpack and shuffled past the family man, looking behind me to see him sitting down within arm's reach of his two little girls. I was pleased with myself and my dedication to sacrifice. A middle seat! But I would endure it. After all, what if my six-year-old was split from me 35,000 feet in the air? It was the right thing to do.

Row 11 is just fine. A business-clad traveling regular on my left is reading a book on Christ filled with frequent blue underlines. On my right sits a millennial with face stubble and worn cargo pants who looks like he may have just returned from hiking in the Andes. They appear two ends of the spectrum of freedom in the world: one to wear a suit on airplanes and prosper with hard work and puritan faith, the other to wander the earth and feel distant landscapes beneath his feet.

Having just departed from a seven-day global academic conference in North Carolina where I represented Wikipedia and the sprawling but loosely organized program I ran within it, I fit somewhere in the middle. Literally, I think, as I buckle my seat belt.

"Where are you from?" blurted a loud man one row behind me in the aisle seat. His voice was louder and more pressured than necessary for casual conversation. The Georgia twang was undeniable. His tenor signaled a lack of restraint or self-consciousness and a charge of self-importance. He was punchy and inquiring, but the slight Asian boy he spoke to—the one immediately behind me—seemed overwhelmed by the volume and enthusiasm.

"I'm from Singapore," he replied. "I finished college and am going back to live with my parents. I, uh, just graduated."

"What did you study?" asked the Southerner.

"Computer science."

"Oh, you must be smart then."

There was a pause, which the drawling commentator quickly filled.

"I'm a scientist, too," the Southerner injected. "Well, I'm not actually a scientist but I oversee scientists. I work on networks, you know the telecommunications backbone. I go into Verizon and T-mobile and make sure everyone's phones work. I'm a problem solver, been doing it for 22 years. I'll tell you one thing, you've got to find work that you like to do, and once you find it, you have to stick with it."

"I have only been on one flight before," the student said. He was wearing a green T-shirt with white lettering. His hair was clipped and had a sweep across his brow to the right. "I am nervous. This is my first flight."

Row 12's window seat was filled with a more mature but equally middle-American fellow who spit chewing tobacco juice into a styrofoam cup.

"Well, if this is your first flight, then how did you get to the U.S.?" he curiously pointed out.

"Oh, then this is my second flight," said the student in a quiet voice.

"So if Singapore is so advanced technologically, why did you come to the U.S. to study?" the Southerner probed, in a nauseating and nativist-sounding line of questioning. I sighed.

I plugged my earbuds into my phone and turned on a droning binaural audio track to drown out the two-sided, pseudo-patriotic interrogation happening behind me.

It was my ninth day of travel, a trip from San Francisco that began with a 40-hour trek to reach Durham, due to weather and the poor decision to make Atlanta a connection hub in disregard for its severe summer thunder and lightning. I got to spend an overnight in Chattanooga, Tennessee, where we'd diverted after the pilot casually announced that if we kept circling Hartsfield-Jackson we'd run out of fuel. It seemed a simple calculation.

I had arrived a day late to my conference and began my campaign of outreach to thousands of professors and administrators. A full week later, eyes closed and trying to zone out to wandering ambient noises, I wanted to finally be home. Through Atlanta. Grab my bags in San Francisco. Drive down the coast to Santa Cruz. I wanted to just have an easy flight, kiss my fiancé, give my six-year-old her presents, and fall asleep in my own bed.

"Sir," the flight attendant said, kindly jostling me from my trance. "Would you like a snack or a drink or anything? It's on us. I feel bad about you having a middle seat. Would you like something to eat or a cocktail?"

I don't usually drink when I fly, but free booze after those dozens of exhibit-hall conversations, evening mingles, company pitches, two-hour lectures, and day-long workshops... well, I guess I deserved it.

"Bloody Mary, please."

She handed me a mini bottle of Tito's handmade vodka and a can of mixer. The briny heat of the drink felt good as I sipped it down. This was guiltless karma. I was being rewarded. This is how the world works: if you are a decent human being, things work out for you in the end. My plastic cup empty down to the remaining cubes of ice, I nestled the drink between my hip and the armrest. I closed my eyes again.

Two minutes later the flight attendant returned. "Would you like one more?" she smiled. "We really appreciate what you did, with the middle seat and all."

I was uncertain but didn't wait for convincing. "OK," I voiced, affirming permission to myself to imbibe again. Karma. Why not?

Behind me the Southerner grated with more tales of his technical exploits. He's always challenged by new technology. He manages a dozen computer engineers. He sees the big picture, how everything fits together. He gets inside the rooms where the servers are—the big ones. His younger friend works for him and his friend is smart—he got the third-highest score on the GREs in the whole country.

Meanwhile, the student is seeming more agitated. "I need to sleep," he says. The Southerner is instantly as helpful as he is boastful and sure. He offers to walk right with the student to the nearest newsstand once we reach Atlanta and show him where the Advil PM is. "Don't worry about it," says the Southerner. "We'll pick you up somethin' PM, no problem."

A few minutes later the student is in pressing discomfort. "I need to pee," I hear him say, as if he has a problem that he doesn't know how to solve. The Southerner seems not one for coddling, but he won't begrudge the young man a guiding hand, and walks him up to the restroom. The student is confused and needs the Southerner to open the inverting bathroom door panels for him. I return to my earbuds.

Behind me I overhear the Southerner and the man with the styrofoam cup confer. "It seems like he's in a bit of a way," says the tobacco-spitter.

The tell-tale signs—anxiety, claustrophobia, fear of flying, intimidation at speaking to two brash Americans, the disorientation of airplanes the first few times you use them—all seem pretty understandable to me.

The student returns awkwardly to his seat. He keeps mumbling something.

"I need peace. I need to sleep. I need to sleep. I need to sleep."

A few minutes pass and the student again dislodges from his row, angling towards the rear bathroom in what seems like physical pain. Maybe he is getting sick, I think, or just losing control.

Sitting back, finally I find a rhythm in my music and feel a wave of deepening dissociation overcome me. I welcome the tendrils of naptime as I start to slip into my subconscious. It is a moment of respite I have been dreaming of for days. Zoning, droning, sinking into my seat. It is blissful. I lose track of time.

"CODE RED" says a tense voice over the loudspeaker. I jerk upright and for a millisecond scan the plane for a burning engine, open escape hatch, or released oxygen mask. There isn't anything wrong that I can see. The passengers are otherwise calm.

I watch a flight attendant walk briskly back towards the bathroom, and put my earbuds back in. "I guess he threw up or had a panic attack," I say to the hiker on my right before turning up the volume.

"Are there any doctors on the plane?" an urgent voice sounds out with raised alarm. I look around for hands or movement but no one budges.

A minute later the woman on my side's row-10 window seat reluctantly says to herself, "Well I am a nurse. I guess I better go back there." She's middle-aged, wearing a white blouse and has cropped brown hair. She climbs over two people.

The Southerner is dialoguing in whispers with the tobacco-spitter. I can barely hear them over the engines. "He was in there a long time," the Southerner says. "So, I told them to go and check on him."

"Prepare the airplane for landing," says a voice from the cockpit. It is not the pleasant airplane voice that beckons you to return to Delta with scripted appreciation. He means we are landing now.

The real-time map in front of me shows 25 minutes to our destination. I tell the hiker we must be speeding up into Atlanta, but he's doubtful we made it that far. We didn't even cross the border into Georgia yet, he says.

"Ladies and gentlemen," the pilot continues. "Because of a medical emergency we need to divert."

Another flight attendant hurries towards the rear of the plane with a large blue bag I suspect is filled with medical supplies. Heads turn to catch a glimpse of what is happening but from row 11 there is only speculation.

The tobacco-spitter is raising concerns—that boy didn't seem in his right mind. He kept getting upset, saying those things about his needs—peace. And sleep. The Southerner agrees, something wasn't as it should be.

A blonde flight attendant comes by row 12 to speak with both men behind me. Her eyes are bloodshot, and though her voice is steady, there is wetness welling up to her eyelashes. She asks the Southerner what happened. He summarizes, as the tobacco-spitter notes his observations in alternating statements.

The plane corrects suddenly to the left and we are tipped downward to descend. The town we are flying over is filling out to the edges with flat green spaces. This is not Atlanta.

We touch down and taxi quickly towards the gate. We can see a fire truck and an ambulance, red lights blinking.

"Ladies and gentleman," the pilot begins again. "Please remain seated while the paramedics board the plane."

Four men, well-built, confident, eyes flooded with focus and adrenaline, careen down the aisle towards the missing student. I wait. People around us are playing guessing games. Realizations of missed connections and travel woes catch up with folks who start calling their airline representatives amid the event.

I am beginning to grasp something more serious than flight delays. The Southerner is upset and signalling something worse than fainting or puking all over the toilet. He can't say what but he is fixated on the student's state of mind. "'I need sleep, I need sleep' he just kept sayin'."

A shuffle of eight footsteps overtakes row 11 as the men in their dark blue uniforms go by us in the opposite direction. Each has a hand on a sturdy sheet corner. Inside is something heavy, its still weight dragging along the airplane carpet. I see two knees wobbled over to one side. I cannot see a face.

A flight attendant returns to row 12 and asks the two interlocutors if they can write down their reports. She is still weary-eyed and starting to lose that crisp facade of seasoned airplane personnel. She is looking far too human for the incessant demands of this work. Something seems broken.

A minute later another man in a dark blue uniform walks past us. This one has a gun on his hip and a badge. Suddenly it all hits me. Like a battering ram in the gut. Police don't investigate seizures and stomach aches. They investigate deaths.

I feel the energy spilling out of my intestines like someone has released a ballast of my spirit. I know the smell of death, from long-loved puppies put to sleep, to hospitalized pill-swallowers who barely escape overdoses. It is a scent that ties empty knots inside you and grips at your breath.

In the unclear moments afterwards, we are left in purgatory on the tarmac. There is no news of when we can continue to fly. Gossip spreads, and with my row 11 middle seat position between the row 12 Americanos and the row 10 nurse, I am well-placed to collate and corroborate details.

He was in the bathroom for over 15 minutes. They found him on the floor. He wasn't moving. There were signs, ones you can't unwash from memory, *that he had done it to himself.*

We are given permission to exit the plane and seek out our final destinations with rental cars or new flights. The plane thins out, but many of us are stranded, wanting for further details. Atlanta is inundated with more thunderstorms and nothing is landing there anyway. We wait.

Another policeman boards the plane. Then an air marshal. It feels like the signature is being put on the documents. Final confirmation. Time of expiry.

A flight attendant hunches over at row 10 and speaks with the nurse. They discuss equipment and procedure. "You really should have an EpiPen," the nurse says. "And glucose."

"I know," says the attendant. "I will bring it up at my next training. And CPR, this new method of 60 pumps per minute is too hard."

"It should be 30 pumps per minute," the nurse agrees. "It's all about the breath. These new recommendations for just pumping and no breaths is not the best."

I learn that CPR in the rear of a five-seat wide plane is difficult. There's no good angle to get at the sternum. Arms tire. I learn the student was long and his body barely laid flat in the tight spaces. I learn that atropine and adrenaline were administered by the paramedics. I learn the student remained unresponsive.

More minutes go by in static agony. The flight attendant returns to the nurse from the front of the plane.

"They have a heartbeat," she affirms.

I think this is good news, but I see in both their eyes that this is definitive of nothing. Hearts can beat when brains have long given up their grasp on the body.

"Well at least there's a heartbeat," the nurse says, sounding more resigned than relieved.

We take off an hour later in the same plane. The weather had cleared in Atlanta and we could land, then scamper towards new airplanes or baggage claim carousels. On the flight there I use the bathroom. Inside I wonder whether it's this one I'm in on the left, or the other one across, where they found him lifeless. Where he decided he couldn't go on. I think about what kind of pain, sickness, fear, or dejection he must have been suffering.

I think about how I am lucky to be feeling strong enough to console the teary flight attendant as I walk back in the plane. How I could tell the nurse how thankful we were for her. How the tobacco spitter should feel reassured that he did everything he could.

I learn that he told the student he would be fine, didn't need to do nothin' but put his head back and relax, and showed him pictures of his kid who graduated college to take his mind off of things. I ask him how he is doing.

"I'm in shock I guess," he says. "Really, thank you for asking, brother."

I think more about the distance I have traveled to and from the cliffs and beaches of Santa Cruz. How each flight was one more travail and delay and detour from getting to my destination and making it back safely. I think about the student's parents, about going home. About how some people take off, and never get there.

Everything described above happened, though I've changed some details to protect the identity of the victim and those involved.

Liminal

There is a space between my words and your flesh
I can still smell after you left.
What I can't remember is the thing you said
That made me burn inside
With laughter and shame.
Beyond the walls snow was falling,
Silent flakes dropped to the ground.
Now that you are gone I wander through the roots of oak trees,
Looking for pieces of myself that used to fit together.

It's been 13 years and my heart still whirrs
Like a crankcase needing oil.
The sound of my own blood pumping is enough to
Drive one mad
It did in fact.
But I ran just quickly enough to stay ahead of each lub,
So far and fast that my own bones fell out of my body
And my remains skirted along the dirt in a sharp wind.
Long after I thought I knew where I was going,
The breeze had taken my skin aloft in a desperate flurry.
There was nothing left to feel the feelings I died to flee.
Except in the morning, once again I could hear your breathing
The lingering whisper of your gently rising chest
And a voice I struggled to place, less forget.

Nobody knows this story, because I burned it
And milled the ashes into
Paste for lining the bindings of broken books.
Now they read of my history
Unknowingly brushing past
Each moment, an epoch that lies between the fossil layers
Waiting to be discovered or subsumed into some inky gold.

I'd still trade it all for one word,
One brush of your cheek against the paper of my mouth,
One drop from your cracked quill.
If you would give me just that
I would leave you alone all over again.

Sex and Sanity

A vagina is the greatest cul de sac in the world. It's a nice place to raise a kid.

A mental institution is the worst cul de sac in the world. There's only one way out but everyone is still lost.

We all get into a cul de sac the same way. At some point, we got fucked.

A baby knows there's only one exit to a cul de sac. But it still gets stuck if it goes breech. If it tries to get out feet first. You can't get out of a mental institution that way. You can't just walk out. You have to go head first. Change something about the way you think.

Another way a vagina is like an asylum is when you leave a lot of shit comes up.

Everyone looks at you in wonder to see if you're still breathing. And then smacks you to make sure you're alive. And for all the pain you caused them.

If you're Jewish after you're born they wait eight days and then cut the top of your penis off. No wonder we're neurotic. Your best friend in the world takes your hat off in the middle of a blizzard and chucks it into a crevasse. It's tradition.

When I got out of the mental hospital I wrote a lot of comics. I drew one person but two thought bubbles. Writing is a lot like that. You're having a conversation with yourself and waiting to see if anyone responds.

I like vaginas a lot more than I like mental institutions. The more time I spend in one the more I want to go back. Not mental hospitals. Once was enough.

The late genius writer David Foster Wallace wrote a famous essay called "A Supposedly Fun Thing I'll Never Do Again." Mental hospitals are "A Supposedly Terrible Thing That Precisely Lives up to Its Reputation."

You shouldn't be afraid of a mental institution though. Of treatment. A vagina, an asylum, a cul de sac. It's a safe place. A great spot to grow up. But you can't live there forever.

Wherever you are, it's okay to be crazy.

After all, nobody knows why we're here. Nobody.

Everyone is here and nobody knows where "here" is or what it's for.

I think that's crazy.

If you stick your penis inside a vagina and rub back and forth until it explodes that makes a baby and civilization continues.

It's delicious, but also crazy.

I'd never commit suicide. Unlike a cul de sac there's no coming back. It's just a going. Where? Nobody know that either.

But I'd rather be crazy here than not be crazy there.

Welcome to the Circle

I had the chance to sit down with a group of amazing people and hear their stories. Before we started we laid out some ground rules. This is what we agreed to…

1. Listen. It's the only and most important thing you have to do. To listen fully is powerful and empowering.

2. Don't judge. Make this a safe space.

3. Details of who was here or who said what are not for sharing outside this room. Repeating general or sufficiently anonymous things you learned is okay. Talking specifically about your own experience afterwards is often helpful.

4. It's brave to share. It's not required. It's always okay to say "I'd rather not talk about it."

5. You are free to leave at any time.

6. Every type, stage, or severity of situation or condition is relevant. Your feelings and emotions are not in competition with others.

7. We're here to support, not to diagnose or prescribe.

8. If you need to cry, that's okay.

9. Anger is a healthy emotion and not something to be ashamed of.

10. Humor is great, if you're speaking about your own experience.

11. It's always okay to seek, ask for, and receive help.

12. Some conditions are temporary. Some require continual monitoring and maintenance. Some go away but then come back. Bring whatever you're dealing with, wherever it falls on your path.

13. Some people take medications, others don't. Neither is right or wrong—it's whatever works for you.

14. Your experience is unique. Your story matters.

15. You are not solely defined by mental health, but you may be relieved, strengthened, or enriched by addressing it.

16. Parts of what you struggle with may be tied to parts of what make you great. It's about the degree of disruption or wanting to change something that determines if it is a problem.

17. Just because you feel or do some of the same things as others doesn't automatically mean you have their condition. If someone's story resonates with you, that's important. At the same time, it just raises nerves to think everyone else's challenges are what you have to solve in yourself.

18. You don't take on responsibility for the health of others who share. You can be an ally. You can ask if people are okay. You can show compassion. But don't take on the burden of fixing each person, and do remember just how valuable listening can be.

19. Outside the room, ask permission to re-engage. "Do you mind if I ask you about…" is a good way to respectfully bring up a conversation in between circles. It's okay to finish a

circle and not want to discuss it again until the next time; it's okay to keep some things just for, and just during, a circle.

20. Learn from each other. Share your tips. "What worked for me…" is a lovely starting point. "What worked for you?" is a fantastic question.

21. Mental health carries a powerful stigma. The more we are open about it, the less that weighs all of us down.

22. Keep in mind that specific intent to seriously harm yourself or others has to be confidentially reported. This is not a threat against you, but a protection for your safety and a chance for you to be professionally evaluated. For clarity, merely thinking about self-harm or wanting to self-harm is not the same as currently self-harming or planning to self-harm. Saying you feel like hurting someone isn't the same as actually hurting or planning to hurt someone.

23. You don't always feel better right after sharing. It can take time to unwrap, unravel, process, digest, reflect, and integrate. Give yourself that time.

24. There is surprising strength, beauty, power, and clarity in the trust and vulnerability of sharing and listening.

25. Gratitude is a gift: *Welcome to the Circle*. Thank you for being here.

How to Save Someone's Life Or Just Get Them into Therapy (Part 1)

I was involuntarily hospitalized for anxiety and "mood weirdness" eight years ago. I had refused every attempt to help me up to that point. But once I was trapped in a facility for two weeks, I decided to try some new things. Since then I've had an unexpected but satisfying run of, ironically, helping other people get into therapy. I have some tips in case you ever encounter this situation. There are no guarantees, but it may make a difference.

Step 1: Let people come to you
- Why will they do this? They will come to you more if you have successes but don't hide behind them, if you share your struggles, show that weaknesses are human, and believe that we're inherently worthy but also capable of growing. Hint: this is also a good way to live freer and happier yourself.
- If someone doesn't come to you but you are concerned, lightly reach out and ask them how they are doing. If they don't bring up an issue with you, they're probably not ready. If you do think it's important to bring it up, do so as non-confrontationally as possible: "I really don't mean to pry but I was wondering if you were having a hard time, and I wanted you to know that I would be happy to just listen and not judge." If they decline, don't push. Just say, "OK, no problem, I just want you to know that I'm here if you ever want to talk."

Step 2: If they want to talk, 99.9% just LISTEN
- You might feel like you don't know what to say: remember that you don't need to say anything to be helpful. Listening is extremely powerful. Just keep gentle eye contact and go

mmhmm or nod every few sentences. Be patient and present.
- An effective response to give is to empathize through reflecting. "That sounds hard." "Wow, that sounds really hard." "It sounds like it's been really hard to deal with this for a long time." "So what I'm hearing you say is [insert what they just told you] is hard for you." This is called "active listening", and it's a simple, highly-underused technique of human communication.

Here are some general DO's and DON'Ts...
- DON'T minimize their problem. ("Everyone goes through this" or "You're making a big deal out of nothing" or "It's all in your head.")
- DO praise the sharing itself. Tell them you're really glad they told you about what they're going through. It really is brave. Encourage and reassure them it was okay to share.
- DON'T try to solve their problem for them. Don't become their therapist. You're doing a lot—and enough—just by listening. Your goal is not to make their problem your problem.
- DO give a particular kind of personal reflection. Highly personalized, as in: "What worked in my life, for me, and this is just my story, it may not work for you... [was to find someone I could talk to a few times confidentially and with no pressure or expectations]."
- DON'T make direct comparisons to your own issues. Don't go into great detail about your own experience, or turn the conversation around to be about you. And don't one-up someone's pain or trauma. You don't know what it's like for them, and everyone's struggle is meaningful by itself.

Step 3: Offer to help get them help
- The best way to offer help is to ask for permission to help (even, "Would it be okay if I offered to help you?"). Asking

permission for very small steps makes people feel like they can control the pace. It reduces anxiety and pressure.
- Accept that they might not want help, at least not yet. People's journeys are long and sometimes they're not ready. "No" is an acceptable answer. So is "Leave me alone."** Maybe they're okay with where things are, or are getting help already, or trying something themselves.
- To explore, help them consider options by asking unloaded questions ("Do you think you would feel better if you talked to someone privately?", "Is there something you're struggling with about the idea of therapy?"). Exploring options and doubts is helpful and adds perspective without pressure. Often people are afraid of therapy, and that's normal.
- If you can, reduce anxiety about therapy itself. Emphasize that therapy is on their terms. They get to share what they want when they want. They don't have to talk about anything. They're in charge of how they get help. Also, whether or not to take medication is a decision they get to make.**

Step 4: Hold their hand to the hand-off

- If someone is depressed, anxious, or in emotional distress, the first step is often the hardest. Ask permission to check in with them after a day or a week—and then check in with them. If they don't respond, don't add pressure or escalate.** If they respond but they haven't made any moves, ask if they're stuck and, again, for permission if you can help.
- Handle logistics. Finding a therapist or doctor and getting an appointment is a lot of work for someone who is struggling emotionally or with their mental health. Offer to look up nearby doctors, phone numbers, insurance policies, etc. Keep a light but steady hand involved until there is an

appointment, or until they express that they think they can take it from there.

Step 5: Follow up
- Check in again a few weeks later. How are they doing? Did they make or go to an appointment? Don't ask for details, just tell them you hope they get some relief, or whatever they're looking for.
- Once a person is getting help, don't assume they'll ever want to talk about it with you again. You did a great job. Feel proud. Let them be as they are, unless they want to talk more. Also, if you don't want to talk more, it's always okay to say, "I don't think I can help any more right now."

Step 6: Keep confidentiality, with an escape valve
- When someone entrusts you with their pain or problems, it's a special bond. Keep it safe and sacred.
- HOWEVER, and this is where the stars** come in… it is not only okay but absolutely necessary to tell someone in a position of responsibility if you think the person is an immediate danger to themselves or others. Note that there's a difference between having "suicidal/violent feelings or thoughts" and "suicidal/violent intent to act". The difference is not always clear, but generally turns when there's a plan, a timeline, and/or if they are dangerously no longer in control of their own behavior. If you're unsure, ask a professional or emergency service.
- Remember that helping someone still doesn't make their problem yours. And many things are out of your control no matter what you do.

Last, having problems is normal! They're often temporary and resolvable. You might even have some one day! Therapy doesn't mean you're sick or broken, but it is a safe and very cool way to air your burdens.

And, you never have to do any of this. It's your free will, your boundaries, your journey. But you may one day face a situation where you want help, or you are the one responsible for helping. If that ever happens, I hope this helps.

Convenience

I spent the nights at a 24-hour gas station
The lights were bright
Even at 3:37am
The magazine rack was stocked
and I read every one
There were hot dogs on rollers
And well
they were cheap
There were packs of almonds
and single-serving cheese
Fountain refills cost 50 cents
but they didn't mind
The bathrooms were always clean
The newspapers delivered on time
There were two tables
where you could read the comics
Or rest your head
like on an airplane

There was another man who came in like me
He had long gray hair
and he said he was Jesus

Jesus had been a lawyer
in a life before
We argued about politics, and Israel
I tried to convince him that Muslims
weren't that bad
Until he took his stack of scripture
And went back into the hills to sleep
under trash bags and blankets in the snow

Some night the local paper said
he snuck into an unlocked cabin
and slept on their flannel sheets

At trial his defense was simple
Surely Jesus deserved
a warm house
On the merits
it was persuasive
But property trumps prophecy these days
and he was convicted

One morning at the gas station a woman
started screaming at the cashier
irate her coupon didn't get her
a free pack of cigarettes
I got up and stood by the counter
Watching closely
"That's enough"
I said
She seethed
and walked off in a huff
The employee thanked me
I sat back down to finish the International section

Any place can be a home
and you have to protect it

A Eulogy for Paradon

The last days of Paradon Munro were not like the first.

Born in Thailand, he was left under a bridge in a cardboard box. When he was three days old, police found him. He was dying. He needed surgery, so he was taken to a police hospital for a primitive operation that left him with a jagged scar.

Don, as he came to call himself during his middle years, was moved to an orphanage. He never knew who his parents were. He grew up among other children, sitting on cushions in the heat of the day under fans blowing down humid air. At an early age he was taught to listen, observe, and be present.

Some years later a couple visited Thailand looking to adopt. They were western, cosmopolitan, well-educated, political, entrepreneurial, and socially unlike the privileged but sheltered suburban parents in Philadelphia's posh Main Line towns where I grew up. Don moved into their sprawling colonial house just a minute's walk away from the famed Barnes Museum.

I met Don before I knew him. I was the pitcher in our Little League team, known for my consistent fastballs right down the plate. Don was the catcher. He would bend, lunge, and dive, using his body to stop my throws in any way and to defend home base from invaders. He was strikingly alert but virtually silent.

I played soccer, and he played soccer. I decided to join the wrestling team, and he decided to wrestle too. In those days he asked to spend time at each other's houses. I usually went to his, a foreign place with strange pieces of international art, an obedient black Labrador, and lots of empty rooms.

Don had an iconic poster of Bruce Lee on his wall and aspired to be like him in the way one sculpts oneself into the image of an idol. Don was short and had tan skin, was nearly hairless, and cultivated a martial-artist-like physique. He was toned and strong in a way that most kids are not.

One afternoon Don cajoled me into trying something. He took a goopy substance wrapped in a green leaf and microwaved it. I was hesitant but at his urging tasted for the first time banana sticky rice with black beans. It was his favorite treat from Thailand. It was new and good.

Don had an interesting and diverse collection of hobbies that intrigued me, and a way of studying them that seemed to surpass my casual tinkering. One afternoon Don and I went biking. He had a set of tools with which he could fix gears and replace tires. I barely knew the rules of traffic, and Don chastised me when I went through an intersection without checking for cars turning right into my lane. He knew things in a more worldly and concrete way than I did. I was used to wandering around random cul de sacs with no particular aim.

Our worlds collided most on the wrestling mat. Don lacked talent, but he was hardened and hard-working beyond his peers. I was busy learning advanced maneuvers while Don was stuffing my head in the mat, showing me that I hadn't mastered the basics.

Don began to emerge as more confident. He attended wrestling camps and developed an arsenal of moves I had not seen before. His conditioning was unparalleled, and his intensity could be fierce. I had an advantage though: he was just 120 pounds and I had been growing and lifting weights. I could toss him off balance when I wanted to, but he continued to put me through drills that made my head sore. "Come on," Don would say as he sought more from me in one arena or another.

Between semesters Don spent a summer in Thailand, living and working on a rice farm. He spent the day studying the genetics of different variants of grain and still made time to jump rope under the hot tropical sun.

During student government elections for our last term in high school Don decided to run for class Secretary. I was a three-time returning Treasurer and had prepared a noble but trite oration about vision and cooperation. Don stepped in front of the audience, and in a flash of bravado, tore off his warm-up pants and removed his t-shirt to reveal a taut black wrestling singlet. He gave a rousing speech to the crowd who cheered him on.

Before college Don joined AmeriCorps and was placed in a poor minority school. He volunteered to become the wrestling coach, biking 45 minutes to school each way, even after a grueling session on the mat. I don't know what the kids learned about takedowns, but Don sat them all in a circle after their workout and talked to them about values, integrity, and how to grow into a good person.

We had left for different schools. I attended Wesleyan University in Connecticut and he went to Franklin & Marshall College in Pennsylvania. We both wrestled our freshman year. Don became a driving, young leader on his team. I became quickly disillusioned with the inane locker room banter, and with the stifled pace of grown muscle interfering with my seasoned tricks. Don wrestled for four years. I dropped out of the team after the freshman season to practice yoga postures and visit the gym when I felt like it.

After college Don moved to Asia where he could hone his first language and become a businessman in global shipping and logistics. I went west to Colorado and started a tutoring company in the groomed mountains of Vail and Aspen.

Don would call me from time to time and try to talk. He would always ask, "Are you happy?"

In Thailand Don earned respect, and became a successful manager at a large company selling the pride of his homeland's harvest. He met a wonderful guy from Nepal. They fell in love.

When our high school wrestling coach, who had been crippled with advanced diabetes, finally passed away, it was Don who wrote a eulogy for him in the town paper. He showed gratitude and maturity in his recollections.

Then one sunny morning in Santa Cruz, at 34 years old, I saw a ping on Facebook.

Don had a stroke. Don was dead.

The comments streaming in recalled a person of unfailing politeness and positivity. Someone who showed up well around everyone he met. There was shock and sadness at the tragedy of it. At a life cut short.

An email came to my inbox, written by his family. "We lost a dear son, life partner, and wonderful man. Please gather with us to pray and honor our beloved Paradon, who left us so suddenly."

Don was like a shadow in my life. A constant coach I never hired but learned from throughout my youth. He kept rousing me, even when I would rather have been dreaming. Don's message was no less than Benjamin Franklin's charge to us: "Up, Sluggard, and waste not life; in the grave will be sleeping enough."

What do we do with loss? How do we grieve and make sense of something so senseless? I remembered Don's words. I had to return to reality and face it even when he could no longer speak them. I had to lean on what I still knew. What did I know about Don?

Don lived with intention and ferocity. Don pushed those around him to be stronger. Don didn't regain consciousness. Don died this week.

But he wasn't alone—and he was happy when he went.

If I Can Make It

- If I can use industrial trash bags filled with newspapers as a urinal in my mountain cabin
- If I can hose out the floor of my mountain cabin because even industrial trash bags leak
- If I can sleep through a Colorado winter in my Subaru using the car's heater for warmth
- If I can clean porta-potties with a power washer and suction hose as a temp worker in the Rockies' summer sun
- If I can drive on the highway with a broken radiator and pull off five times each mile to cool down
- If I can use shoes to cushion my elbows when I sleep on a tiled bathroom floor
- If I can make 8 dollars cleaning a gas station scrubbing the hot dog rollers and cleaning the restrooms
- If I can wash one set of clothes for the week while taking a shower at a local pool
- If I can come out of my room only from 3am to 5am when everyone in the house is asleep
- If I can cover my entire body in Vaseline so I don't have to feel the frigid air on an outing in December
- If I can use bubble gum to plug my ears so I don't have to be overwhelmed by conversation at a family party
- If I can cover an air conditioner with a Listerine-soaked towel to mask the smell of my bedroom
- If I can get arrested for failing to appear in court for a traffic ticket right after calling the police on my abusive housemate
- If I can eat only discount convenience store trail mix for an entire week
- If I can spend the night in a jail cell with a man going through withdrawal speaking about demons in Spanish
- If I can look up Wikipedia articles about my intrusive thoughts to reassure myself I'm not a delinquent abuser

- If I can shovel snow wrapped in a fleece blanket because I refuse to wear a real winter jacket
- If I can ask the barista four times if my latte is decaf because I think regular coffee will render me a cheater at my life
- If I can use newspaper to insulate my shoes while doing demolition on a brick building in the freezing morning
- If I can shave at the mental hospital with an attendant watching so no one cuts themselves on purpose
- If I can stay up for 36 hours and sleep for the next 24
- If I can not wake up for breakfast until 9pm
- If I can have dinner of 10 slices of bread and a stick of butter
- If I can get scolded for standing on a bench for the last two minutes of sunlight before going back into a mental hospital
- If I can argue that my friend lacks flexibility because he's upset I'm wearing my pants inside out in public
- If I can move into a new apartment and never unpack my things for two years
- If I can pay for a storage locker to hold my belongings for four years, run out of money, and have it all auctioned off
- If I can rent an apartment for two months, and pay for it, but be too afraid to ever move in
- If I can think that the flicker of a raised eyebrow from my best friend over dinner is a crushing and unforgivable insult
- If I can not brush my teeth for three years and lose only one tooth
- If I can get so frustrated that I punch the wall behind my attic hallway so many times the drywall just crumbles
- If I can lock my parents out of my room using three rigged-up bungee cords
- If I can befriend a homeless alcoholic and let him sleep on the bunk bed in my cabin while he gets medications for his anxiety
- If I can get to know the two cashiers at a local market and be invited over to their house for homemade rice and beans

- If I can crash on the couch of a Jamaican immigrant and become a surrogate father to her one-year-old son
- If I can get surprise visits from my five college friends to have at least one day a season where I come out of my cave
- If I can keep balance and stay on five different psych medications
- If I can leave my car, keys, and title in a random parking lot and decide to fly home for an uncle's funeral—instead of languishing in remote purgatory

If I can make it through all of this... then whatever you're going through, you can make it through too.

Stonefruit

The truth hurts
the way you put insight inside bombshells
or wrap bow ties on daggers
something doesn't match
and it scares me
to my liquid core

Your truth hurts
it makes me fear the razor stuffed in the peach
or the lemon-scented baton

I'm nauseous from the pain
of not knowing whether
to slap back your face
or say thank you

Maybe next time you can wash truth in a basin
pick off each of its gnarly thorns
render palatable the nectar
so I can eat again
and be nourished

I like the sound of that

You won't though
you'll keep assaulting me with rocks of wisdom
that smash in my forehead
trying to make your point
and it will kill me
but it will make me stronger

You can't control it
pick the pearls from the shell

untie the knotty mess
truth doesn't come like a gentle rain
it tears off your roof
and lets you see the passing storm
cracking boulders in the atmosphere

I need the noise
to shudder me awake
to rouse me from delusion
so like a tumultuous angel
you break me open

I honestly don't care for it
but if I listen
I can hear a cacophony of love

I like the sound of that

Still I fantasize about
a sieve for all the hailstones
but is there enough metal in the earth
and how would it hang
it makes me laugh just thinking about it
who would build such a contraption
only a dreamer
who likes the sound of that

So pray tell me one more time
what it is you had to say
please be patient
spread out your thunder
let me catch my breath
and swallow the sky

How to Save Someone's Life Or Just Get Them on Medication (Part 2)

Though it nearly always helps, therapy may be neither necessary nor sufficient for recovery.

In my mental health journey, two years before I was hospitalized, I started twice-a-week sessions with a seasoned and solid therapist. Our conversations would be winding and erudite, free-wheeling and spirited. And then I would crack.

It could be a single word he said. Or an analogy I didn't prefer. The title of a book on his shelf. A vibe he emanated. Or just the rising of an emotion I couldn't tolerate or permit. Then I would freeze in tears and barely speak the rest of the hour. We lengthened our sessions to give room for recovery but it just kept happening.

Finally, he suggested to me, in the mildest way possible, that medication might help.

I didn't want that. He knew I didn't want that. He knew I needed it. I refused to even consider.

While sustained talk therapy is one of few proven "drugs", it can be extremely hard to do at all, or comfortably, or sustainably—if uncontrollable emotions, compulsions, flashbacks, and fears are dominating the session.

You may think therapy is precisely the place for such happenings, and it's partly true. But therapy doesn't always feel sufficiently safe, or what it unearths cannot be contained between the appointments, or it raises new angers and pains that simply overwhelm. There is a reason medication and therapy repeatedly show optimal efficacy when paired: therapy can be hard and medication can make it more tolerable and rich.

So what do you do if someone you love or care for is resisting medication, either alone or as part of treatment? Here are 16 tips to guide you.

1. **Talk about resistance.** I don't mean call out a person's resistance to medication as to cast blame. I mean acknowledge they don't want to take medication. State it plainly: "I see and hear that you're against taking medication." Try to find out why. Did they take meds before and feel like a zombie? Were they forced to take meds while hospitalized? Are they afraid of side effects like weight gain or grogginess or sexual dysfunction? Are they terrified they'll lose their emotions and become numb? Do they think it makes them weak or a failure, and that they should be able to figure it out on their own? Are they embarrassed others will think they are sick and stigmatize them? Do they worry they'll be on meds their whole life? Did they try medications before in a traumatic context and now associate medications with that trauma? Did they try medication before and it just didn't help their anxiety or depression or psychosis or PTSD? Are they afraid they won't be themselves on meds or that meds will irreparably change their personality? Once you know more you can tailor your response. But take their resistance as valuable data. Your goal, at least at first, is not to change their mind but to understand it.

2. **Share your own prescription.** The best evidence is testimony. If you now or ever before took psychiatric drugs, then have the courage to share that. If you can, be specific about when you started taking them, what you take them for, how they help, how you manage side effects, what you worried about and what you learned. If you don't or didn't take these drugs but know someone who has, share that too. Be clear that you don't

judge them for it. Stigma hates company and is felled by wholehearted acceptance.

3. **Don't prescribe.** You're not a doctor and don't need to be. Leave the details to professionals and let the person you're talking to keep an open menu of options. Meds that worked for one person may not work for another. Meds are very personal and require direct experience to evaluate.

4. **Never threaten.** Unless someone is an immediate danger to themselves or others and you plan to force their arrest or hospitalization, DO NOT turn medication into a weapon for leverage. That's a threat you may only get to make once.

5. **Look at alternatives.** Try to frame meds as a choice the person gets to make. "I see you're against medications, and I see you're struggling right now. What if you had more buffer from the pain and more tools to work on what you want?" Resistance is ultimately a vote for the status quo. Don't push, but do mention realities in which their symptoms are lessened or their options multiplied.

6. **Promote experimentation.** No one who takes a medication has to stay on it. It would be crazy to permanently commit to an unknown remedy with no exit or ability to adjust. Taking psych meds is really a process of trial and sometimes error. Not in the sense that the patient is a lab rat, but in the way that an artist combines colors to see what looks good together. Taking psych meds is a process of trying, evaluating, and adjusting. The patient is a critical part of this: they know how they feel, what they do or don't like, what they can or can't tolerate, and how their thoughts or behavior is impacted.

7. **Remember the variable of time.** Even the best drugs can take weeks or months to reach their full effect. Xanax may work

in minutes while Risperdal takes weeks and Prozac takes months. Before that time passes, you can't really judge if something's working. Even then, "working" depends not only on the drug but also on all of the feelings and behaviors associated with taking it. That can take time to reveal. Once on a stable regimen, conditions, challenges, and chemistry may change. A person could need more or less meds, different meds, or no meds at all. Time is a key ingredient.

8. **Consider side effects.** If I gave you a cigarette and told you it would kill you in 40 years, you might still smoke it. If I gave you one and told you you would gain 20 pounds, lose your energy, feel brainless, not be able to orgasm, and have constant thirst or twitching, you might not. Psych meds can have very real side effects. Don't pretend otherwise. Do emphasize that the main effects of reducing symptoms often outweigh the drawbacks. Side effects are manageable whereas symptoms often are not. Also, side effects are data about what drugs or doses are working or need to be tweaked. It's not an immediate process; a psych doctor is looking for the best meds in the right amount with the right combinations at the right time.

9. **Seek effective not numb.** One of the most common, and valid, objections to psych meds is that they will make you feel dulled, muted, monotone, and a shell of yourself. Emotional variability can be excessive or problematic, but people still prefer it to emotional silence. At least if a person is feeling, they have a sense of self and that they are alive. If they are totally numb they might as well not be. Be sensitive to the desire to preserve self and emotion, even if a person's sense of self is distorted or their emotions are out of control. Emphasize that the purpose of meds is not to erase a person, but to lower the volume of whatever is disturbing them and getting in the way of their genuine pursuit of happiness and improvement.

10. **Minimal effective dose.** Like a physical joint that is injured, the goal of taking meds is not a full-body cast where a simple sling would do just fine. Similarly with psych meds, the goal is the M.E.D.: minimum effective dose. Sometimes in severe cases a doctor will want to strongly rein in risky behaviors, so a more flattening dose might be prescribed at first for safety and to prevent relapse. That is not long-term the goal though, and any good doctor will thereafter experiment with lowering the dose until only its necessary function is performed.

10. **Start small.** Unless someone is under involuntary treatment, there is often no real risk to starting on a minuscule dose and tapering up. While a person might be languishing with no meds at all, they might gain a sense of security and possibility by trying an absolute minimum amount just to demonstrate that meds are not devastating or poisonous to body and spirit. Many meds are intentionally tapered up anyway, so this is often a natural part of the process.

12. **Talk about reducing burdens.** It's really hard being mentally ill. Not just the shame and stigma but the day-to-day experience of life can be disorienting or excruciating. Meds are a way to soothe those symptoms. They can make you feel better. They can make you able to handle life with less pain and distress.

13. **Champion diversity.** Every person has a unique brain. The goal of taking meds is not conformity; it's finding the right balance for each individual. Differences are what make us interesting and often uniquely effective. It's not a goal of meds to erase that special style or approach to life. In terms of basic neurochemistry, the goal of meds is to merely bring neurotransmitters that control feelings of safety, motivation, and self-control into line with a person's needs and aspirations.

14. **Include the whole palette.** Meds are often a keystone of recovery, but emphasize that the best treatments will always be a healthy diet, good sleep, regular exercise, time with friends, laughter, exploring nature, and connecting with the breath. For some people there is a desire to go the "natural" way and avoid meds. Don't make it an either-or false dichotomy. You can take meds and also take advantage of all the tools for health and happiness. Often, taking meds is what permits a person to start using those tools again. It's a jump-start. It's shelter. It's headlights on a windy road. Meds are not prison. The right meds at the right dose empower and free a person.

15. **Define an active role.** Taking medications is just the start of a recovery journey, and the most important person when taking meds is not the prescriber but the patient. When someone takes meds they get to, and need to, advocate for what they want. They get to, and need to, report back regularly on what is working for them and what they dislike. They get to, and need to, express their preferences about the direction they want to go in. They should listen to expertise, but that doesn't mean being a passive object that the meds act on. Meds enable you to act.

16. **Emphasize life.** Each person is on a journey. Often taking meds *feels* like admitting defeat, or like a person is broken. Instead of the injury, focus on the future. Talk about the life they want, and how meds might enable them to have it. They still get to keep their memories, but they have a chance to write the rest of their story.

I couldn't erase what I had been through, but taking meds was the key to unlocking the meaningful pieces that had been missing. It was not taking meds that kept them locked away from me. Meds are like a freshly sharpened pencil in the new chapter of a person's life.

WELCOME TO THE CIRCLE

The Atomic Method

After I stabilized from hospitalization, I made some agreements with myself. I decided, with resoluteness and even a bit of relentlessness, that I would restructure my life towards achieving two goals: I wanted to make Wikipedia a career, and I wanted to build a deep and loving relationship.

Figuring out how to do this was a quest in itself, and I developed a philosophy of accomplishment that helped me get to where I wanted to go. Here's what I realized:

Like an atom's quantum spin, life has two potential versions, two paths it can take. One feels easy and will get you nowhere. The other can make a dent in the world even if you fail.

Version 1: From Acquire to Comfort (don't do this)

"I'm going to get what I want. So in the coming days I'll do something different. I'll do the best things I can do. I'll start lots of new practices that I'll source from many potential ideas. I'll finally become comfortable with who I am."

Acquire: I'm going to get what I want
Tomorrow: In the coming days I'll do something different
Optimality: I will do the best things I can do
Motion: I'll start lots of new practices
Ideas: I'll source from many potential ideas
Comfort: I'll finally become comfortable with who I am

Version 2: From Access to Challenge (do this)

"I'll use all the tools I have, and I have enough space to practice with them now. When good chances arise I'll risk success to shift the dynamics around me. I'll exert myself in the direction I envision, because I want to grow today."

Access: I'll use all the tools I have
Time: I have enough space to practice with them now
Opportunity: When good chances arise, I'll risk success
Movement: To shift the dynamics around me
Influence: I'll exert myself in the direction I envision
Challenge: I want to grow today

Let's break down the differences.

Acquire vs. Access
The first focuses on what you want and receive externally. The second focuses on what you employ and give out internally. Guess which one gets you more? By pouring energy in you make sure you *actually* get out what you want rather than just fantasizing about it.

Tomorrow vs. Time
Anything beyond the day you have now is imaginary, and picturing something being different just because the calendar advances is an illusion. It's easy to think about tomorrow, but then you throw out the most vital resources you have. The 1,440 minutes you have today matter. Realize your imagination by activating the day you have at hand.

Optimality vs. Opportunity
A perfect plan is not the goal of your process. A chance to actually *try* your plan is the real reward which will move you forward, no matter what the result. Optimality is not a starting point: it's the result of experimentation, adaptation, learning, failure, and progress. Get to optimality (or closer to it) by figuring out what works and what doesn't—by trying, testing, and tweaking.

Motion vs. Movement
A list or flurry of potential actions is not the same as committed, purposeful steps. Movement advances you rather than just flailing your energy about.

Ideas vs. Influence
Brainstorming near the end of your process is often just magical thinking in disguise. Instead put your energy towards shifting what is happening to you and around you. Drive to make real change sparks creativity in a way that *serves* your goals. It's not idle brainstorming you're after: connect what's in your head to levers you can pull to get there.

Comfort vs. Challenge
The beginning contains the end. Instead of aiming for eventual comfort, go down the path of immediate change. Realize that your level of comfort is determined by your past actions and your acceptance of where you are now. Comfort tomorrow depends on what you do to grow today. You can have growth without comfort, but you'll never get true comfort without growth.

A.T.O.M.I.C.

This method helped me move forward in my life, by staying focused, keeping positive, and by starting wherever I was, with whatever was available to me. It encouraged me not to wait, and required I be open to trying--not taking failure as a dead end.

I hope the ATOMIC method can help you too:

"I'll use all the tools I have, and I have enough space to practice with them now. When good chances arise I'll risk success to shift the dynamics around me. I'll exert myself in the direction I envision, because I want to grow today."

Haikus

Codependence

You can't help this time.
So how does that make you feel?
It hurts, doesn't it?

We are all alone
And that is your greatest fear:
Can it set you free?

You can only help
The people who are ready.
The rest fall again.

Do you care too much,
Because it masks your own pain?
Do you care for you?

Take care of yourself.
Take care your only true self.
Then you will find peace.

Depression

Did you lose yourself?
In depression there's nothing.
But where did you go?

It hurts just to be.
The excruciating pain
Cannot be escaped.

If you can't feel hope
What's the point of anything?
Why do I go on?

My journey is stalled.
I muddle through every day.
Stuck in misery.

Every day alive
Is a success for your life
We can celebrate.

Borderline

You are everything.
I hate you and I love you;
It kills me again.

My emotions swell
Like a wave crashing on me;
I pray I can swim.

So many insults.
My true friend has gone missing.
Who can I count on?

RAGE RAGE RAGE RAGE RAGE—
LOVE LOVE LOVE LOVE LOVE LOVE LOVE—
TEARS TEARS TEARS TEARS TEARS.

You are suffering
But you can hold together:
Find your true center.

Bipolar

All of a sudden
The joy comes out of nowhere;
I'm myself again.

It crashes as fast.
I'm lower than a fossil
And feel just as dead.

There is thunder but
There is lightning too, and I
Live for the huge storms.

I could be stable,
If I could control these winds.
The sky never stops.

You are more than moods.
Life can be plain and wondrous.
True friends will remain.

Anxiety

Oh, what have I wrought?
What kind of world's so fragile
That needs my fixing?

It will go to pot.
I will fail and fail again.
Life can't be trusted.

What is confidence?
I worry my destiny
Is fearing each day.

It makes me so sad
How much pain will befall us
If I just let go.

Be kind to yourself.
The whole world is not your fault
Try to trust it now.

OCD

"I'm gay! I am gay!
I'm a wretched pedophile!
I'm a murderer!"

That's what the thoughts say.
Who am I to disagree?
Or risk that it's true?

The world will feel right
If I wash my hands enough
Of all of this guilt.

I cannot just stop.
I cannot break my own rules.
I can't fail myself.

Only your brain's stuck.
Break the cycle that tortures.
You deserve freedom.

Addiction

It's only one sip.
Surely I can handle it,
Or am I that weak?

I'd trade everything
To be free of agony,
To feel normal once.

Won't you forgive me?
I never meant to cause harm.
I didn't want this.

My life unravels.
Each day I'm farther away.
How can I come home?

When you realize this:
You can stop and try again,
We wait here with love.

Trauma

All the memories
Hurt when I was just a child
I still feel the pain.

Who can be trusted
If those closest cannot be?
Who can I lean on?

Could the past be changed?
If I could not be afraid
I'd change it myself.

There's nowhere to hide.
I shroud myself in safety
But can't run away.

It was not your fault.
Your now is safer than then.
Find your protectors.

Narcissism

Why don't they see me?
I have to make them see me,
I have to be seen.

If they would listen
My ideas could change the world
Fools never listen.

I am not to blame.
Those mistakes are not my own.
These flaws are not mine.

If you hurt me I'll
Strike back seven times as hard;
You'll pay for it soon.

Be vulnerable.
You can be great, and flawed too.
You're human like us.

Abuse

I am the victim,
Even though I will break you.
I can't not hurt you.

Insecurity
Leads to manipulation.
Don't you understand?

You will get my love.
And when you do, I own you.
You can't argue that.

I hit you again.
I'm sorry you deserved pain.
Don't make me do it.

You must help yourself.
It will take very hard work.
To give love less pain.

Cult

Your truth is not real.
Society is a lie.
But I have answers.

You have brainwashed me.
Family, the enemy
Of my potential.

My past self was false.
Now my new identity
Is revelation.

We can't meet or speak.
You threaten deeper meaning.
Be gone from my world.

If you found the truth,
Then you need not separate.
Truth will survive guests.

Psychosis

The voices just scream.
I'd do anything at all
Just to make them stop.

Do you see my friend?
He visits me at dark times.
But never sees light.

Shadows pass like ghosts.
They are hunting me for sins
I have imagined.

Every day passes
It gets harder to discern
What is in my mind.

Your brain betrays you
What can you believe is real?
Reach out, touch my hand.

Curated Thoughts for Inadvertent Witnesses

1. As in any tragedy, your highest priority is to take care of yourself. Sometimes that happens after taking care of others. It has to happen at some point.

2. Proximity to tragedy is trauma. There is no such thing as an unaffected witness.

3. Our duty in retelling the stories of others' pain is to respect their integrity, dignity, privacy, and memory. A good story cannot supersede that.

4. Effects of trauma can appear days, weeks, months, or even years later. We are first adrenaline-ridden heroes or survivors. When that armor fades, we feel vulnerability with new and sometimes crushing intensity.

5. If you are starting to react to everyday life events like they are loaded, threatening, offensive, or foreboding, it is completely natural. It is also a sign that you need to talk to someone about what happened.

6. Recovery is for the future. We don't examine trauma to solve or cure it, but to make sure that it doesn't derail our own journey towards a meaningful life.

7. When you are weak, lean on the people around you. Literally, go rest your body on someone's chest or shoulder. Just lie there. It's okay.

8. If you can't open to others and you find yourself seeking isolation, then take isolation in self-care. While your mind processes, give your body rest and nourishment.

9. When you are ready, understanding will come. This is not an answer to a question, but a vision for what comes next and a willingness to accept it.

10. Recovery is work. Even when an injury is outside of our control, the task of cleaning wounds falls into our hands. Like much work, it can not only heal but also make you strong. It's okay to become stronger. Sometimes it's the only way.

The Crisis Killing Our Boys

When I was six at Sunday school a boy a year older than me leaned over at snack time and punched me in the stomach. We had been sitting silently next to each other. There was no provocation. It took the wind out of my breath, and I did everything in my control not to show to the rest of the kids that I had been hurt.

When I was eight I was walking home from school and a boy a year older than me spit in my direction from across the street. I spit back, meters away from where he was walking. In seconds he was sprinting towards me, tackled me to the ground, climbed on top of me, and punched me once square in the center of my forehead. I walked the rest of the way home in great distress, not from the pain, but from fear that I wouldn't be able to conceal what had happened.

When I was 12 on a bus ride home from a field trip a boy in my grade turned around and sucker punched me between my eyebrows. He sat back down just as quickly and giggled like it was a harmless prank. I was stunned and didn't say a word. I just sat back down so as not to draw any attention to what had happened.

I wasn't a target for regular bullying—these were just random acts of opportunity. I was smart at school, a fast runner, good at baseball, and popular with the girls. This wasn't being singled out for ridicule and belittling—it was just "what boys do".

In recounting these incidents, I'm most interested in what I did *not* do. Namely, I didn't feel anything—but shame that I had somehow "lost" these encounters. I didn't get angry in response. I didn't cry. I didn't tell someone or ask for help. I didn't react at all, especially externally.

Knowing what I know now, that the fight-or-flight response also has an equally powerful "freeze" alternative, I'm not surprised. But I am deeply dismayed by the aftermath of these events and for what they did not contain. They didn't lead me to seek consolation or comfort. They didn't help me process my bubbling fear or anger. They just receded into that silent book of toxic masculinity that boys take notes in as they grow up.

Growing up, I thought that emotions were for lesser people. I saw friends and family, people I respected, get upset or scared or frustrated. I fashioned myself above these common human reactions. Instead I thought to cultivate a zen-like state in which I lived outside or above these fragile vacillations.

That was a misunderstanding, of both zen and of being human. What I was really doing, with great intent and even pride, was detaching from my feelings, intellectualizing what I was experiencing, and nobly rationalizing away the core of sensing and expressing emotion.

There is a cliff that kids approach when they turn seven. For many girls, this cliff plummets confident, unique, independent, and opinionated beings into a terrible conformity. Fear of hierarchy and status loss, meanness, verbal sniping, preoccupation with physical appearances, and obsession with who the boys like precedes a decade (or far longer) of anxiety about their bodies and their desirability. Books have been written about this "confidence cliff", and the way in which it robs girls of their individuality and robustness.

Less is said about the cliff that many boys face around the same age. Studies show that boys up until the age of seven are actually *more* emotional than girls. They cry more. They are easily wounded, and though sufficiently resilient, both physically and emotionally tender. It is only around this cliff of toughness when boys begin to "suck it up", "act like a man", and "not be a sissy." This is not natural, and yet it is entirely the norm. The *only* emotion left available to young men is anger—the rest is swept off the table and falls to the ground.

When I reached college my first literature course had us read *The Odyssey*. The epic tale of a great and cunning hero left me shocked. In stanza after stanza Odysseus cries. He weeps, wails, and moans. The archetype for Western culture's model man, ceaseless survivor, and adaptable adventurer is near constantly in tears. In an essay for the class, I counted every single time when Odysseus cried. That paper lies in a box in my aunt's basement, but from memory I assure you that there were 100 times when sentimental moods overtook Odysseus and he unleashed a torrent of flowing emotion. No one told him he wasn't manly for it.

> *All his days he'd sit on the rocks and beaches,*
> *wrenching his heart with sobs and groans and anguish,*
> *gazing out over the barren sea through blinding tears.*

In a 2009 convocation speech for Reed College, professor Jan Mieszkowski remarked: "The tough guy code embodied by Hollywood figures such as Clint Eastwood or Vin Diesel is hardly the historical norm. In the Western literary tradition, from *Beowulf* to the *Song of Roland*, from Sophocles and Aeschylus to the modern theater and later the European novel, there are lots of tears shed by big boys with big weapons."

It would be easy to say that toxic masculinity and the trappings of modern patriarchy have robbed "big boys with big weapons" from being able to show their most vulnerable emotions. The same is true of small boys and regular boys and boys who are peaceful and kind.

The Reed professor goes on to say: "By crying, Odysseus loses his identity in the story being told about him, but it is precisely through this loss that he comes into his own as someone who can now tell his own story all by himself. The lust for tears reveals that in the Homeric world desire always has two parts: one hopes to act in a way that will be the basis for a grand narrative of famous exploits; and at the same time, one hopes to act in a way that will not be so easy to fit into the frame of a stable narrative because one desires, perhaps impossibly, to write the story as well as to star in it."

What does it do to a boy who cannot "write and then star in their own story" with their tears?

As I graduated college a torrent of feelings began to stir in me. A close relationship, as turbulent and dysfunctional as it had been intimate and dynamic, overtook my body and psyche. There were sensations I was bombarded with that I could only loosely name let alone process. Hypersensitivity, shame, anger, betrayal, guilt, longing, insult, sadness, desperation, grief, arousal, pity, claustrophobia, irritation, dissociation, anxiety, panic... whirled and caught me in fierce clutches.

I didn't know what to do, so I ran. I simply avoided anything that triggered those overwhelming sensations. I ran from family and friends and places and songs and obligations and memories. Eventually I ran far enough that I wound up back at home living in my parent's attic, sheltered from the world. Then I wound up spending two weeks in a mental hospital for precisely "anxiety and avoidance."

With the help of medications, several of them, I was able to piece back together some stability, and some semblance of boundaries from the onslaught of emotions. What I've done in therapy in the eight years since is learn to slowly unwrap how I process emotions. Like many men, my main framework is intellectual venting. But I've seen its limits. I've had my tenured therapist point out fallacies and narrow frameworks in my thinking. The most important thing she has done is just note when I'm thinking my problems and not feeling them.

When she does this, I pause. It's not that I don't know what she means; it's that I don't know *how* to feel an emotion. She tells me in reassuring tones that our bodies know how to process emotions like they process food or toxins. That we have an emotional system which—if we let it—will move emotions through us. I don't yet know what this means in practice, but I have a hunch that the stoppage in my emotional flow stems back to those earliest years as a boy learning to suppress feelings that I couldn't control, or that would have exposed me as too sensitive for my gender.

Women are generally known for letting their emotions flow (and are often criticized for it). My therapist assures me that women in her practice generally need tissues, while men are just learning how to name the mysterious upwellings in their body and psyche. So I'm exploring what it means to feel an emotion. To let it move. My wife tells me that this process is uncomfortable but brings great relief. Maybe women know about moving through pain, in the way that labor itself is the epitome of a process which gives life through agony. The key is not to shut it down, not to suppress it.

Last month a friend of mine from summer camp committed suicide. He had lost custody of his child in a nasty divorce and couldn't face a future in which he had to live without his son. The grief and the guilt killed him, and he took his own life. When I heard the news I spit out profanities. My wife left the room for a moment. I grabbed a large red pillow and I slammed it as hard as I could against our bed, sobbing so deeply that I barely noticed the gentle hand on my back consoling me. Maybe this was what it was like to feel an emotion. Not a stirring, but a boiling over. "It's OK" she told me, back in the room, "Good job."

When I think back to college, and to Odysseus, I am left with the conviction that what mattered was not that Odysseus cried, but that he cried and still found his way home. Boys need to know, and believe, and have it reinforced that this is okay. They can be heroes with tears. Indeed, they may need their tears to make it home alive.

Before Sean

Stop.
Stop now.
Stop and put down the rake.
Stop or you'll be tasered.
Stop or you'll be shot.
Stop. Stop. Stop.
Shot. Shot.
Life, lost.

There are two truths and a lie.
The truths are:
Sean was ill, mentally ill.
Sean was a threat. He had a large metal rake.
The lie is that he needed to die.

The lie is that police have one tactic,
Stop or I'll…
Shot. Shot.
Collapsed, to the ground.

The lie is that four
trained officers
with tasers
with guns
can be trapped by a parked car.
Can only shout orders.
Can only shoot. Something.
Into bodies.
Stop. Stop. Stop.
Shot. Shot.
Life, gone.

Sean was shot.
Sean was beautiful.
Sean was ill.

Police thinking
fast.
Control the scene.
Command and order.
Tasers.
Bullets.
Blood.
20 seconds.

Police thinking
slow.
There's a man.
He's shouting.
People are scared.
We know he's mentally ill.
We all know it.
You knew it.
You knew it but still all
you could yell was stop.
Stop or I'll…
Shot. Shot.

Next time
there is danger
do not think that you can
kill away an illness.
You can only kill a man.
An illness needs treatment.
Needs patience.
Needs clarity.
Needs time.

But it was raining.
A storm.
Of electrified darts
And bullets.
The rain is not stopping.
Sean is not stopping.
But you must.
Back away.
Avoid the threat.
Contain the threat.
Support the patient.
Help the patient.
Reassure the patient.
Calm the patient.
Requires, patience.

Requires
"Sean,
We're here to help."
"Sean,
You can get help."
"Sean,
We see you suffering."
"Sean,
We're waiting."

To heal this gaping wound.
This life lost.
This child left fatherless.

You are our helpers.
I think you are our helpers.
I need you to be our helpers.
Stop. STOP. Don't shoot.

Sean Smith Arlt was killed by Santa Cruz police on October 16th, 2016. He was the father of a four-year-old boy, the author of a book of poetry called The Love Manifesto, *and a native of Santa Cruz where his parents and brother live and grieve with the community.*

How to Save Someone's Life Or Just Get Them to Stay on Their Medication (Part 3)

Getting *into* therapy and *onto* medications is hard, but this guide looks at what is often even harder: following through and staying on medications through doubts and side effects and temptations to reduce effective treatments.

Let me start with a personal story. I take five psych meds. One is an antidepressant, another two are for anxiety, a fourth for reducing mood downswings, and a fifth for managing mood variability. That is a lot of medications, but for the past eight years, they have helped me develop and sustain a promising career, meet and marry a strong, smart, beautiful woman, and show up for my family and my stepdaughter.

Then one night last month I decided to experiment with lowering *one* of my five medications by *25 percent*. My motivation was that I was planning on eventually coming off this drug, and I happened to be on an exciting romantic retreat with my wife celebrating our two-year anniversary. The medication I wanted to reduce is intentionally *dulling*, as in it lowers sensation and reactivity. But I wanted to experience this weekend to the absolute *fullest*. So the night after we arrived at our campsite overlooking the Pacific Ocean, I dropped from 2 mg to 1.5 mg. I did it without telling my wife or my therapist, because I thought it was within the realm of reasonable experimentation.

The first full day of our trip was marvelous, filled with nature and hiking and scenic vistas and waterfalls. I loved the day. After we returned to camp we enjoyed red wine in camping cups and looked out at the sea. Then we went up to the nearby restaurant for dinner. Perched on the cliff's edge we looked out at whales spouting water and the sun slowly dropping below the red and golden hues of the sky. Then the salad came.

I can't explain in rational terms what happened next, but a visceral disgust overtook me. I was assaulted by the look, the smell, the very presence of that mundane garden salad with its wet cucumbers and shredded carrots, watching my wife pick out pieces of curled lettuce with her fingers, the waft of sickening vinegar dressing. I tried to avert my glance. I felt nauseous. I thought I was going to throw up right on the outdoor deck of the restaurant.

That's what a 25% change in one of five medications did to me. It rendered my senses so *hypersensitive* that it short-circuited any rational sense of stability, and I knew I had gone too far. It terrifyingly reminded me of how life used to feel each day before taking any meds. Fortunately, I still had the insight to admit to my wife what I had tried, and she knew it would be best to return to our sleeping bags and let me calm down. That night I went back up towards my regular dose. Within a few hours I was able to engage. The next day was fine. The following weeks were totally normal. I got lucky.

The temptation, sometimes even the compulsion, to reduce medications is extremely strong. In the following guide I want to look at what you might say to someone doubtful, offering many different perspectives on why *staying* on medication and *not lowering their dose* is often the best option, at least in the short and medium-term, and sometimes for the rest of their happy, healthy, and meaningful life.

1. **Main effects vs. side effects.** One of the biggest complaints with psych meds is what else they do besides reducing the symptoms of a mental illness. Side effects can range from restlessness and insomnia, to fatigue and inability to orgasm, to mental fogginess and weight gain. These are not

trivial, but they need to be put into their proper context. Side effects are called that because they exist alongside *main effects*, the reduction of primary symptoms. Main effects can include stopping or reducing suicidal thoughts, debilitating anxiety, delusions, and wild mood swings. People on medications often fixate on side effects and forget that those side effects only arise because you are addressing the real, deeper, underlying problem. It's the main effects that are most critical, and side effects must be a secondary consideration in serious mental illness.

2. **The three diseases.** Mental illness is actually a trio of challenges. First, there is the original condition, the compilation of symptoms that destabilized and endangered a person. Second, there is the challenge to accept the disease and stop denying it exists or believing it will just go away. Third, there is the desire and even obsession with lowering meds and effectively reducing or stopping treatment for the main condition. Any consideration of a person's mental health needs to look at all three components, because they work in tandem and you often fail when they're not in sync.

3. **Rejecting the main symptoms.** A person who is on treatment for a mental health condition often comes to reject the symptoms that brought them to treatment in the first place. The negative mental chatter, the self-harm, the irrational fears, or distorted hallucinations—once properly treated with meds—become a source of myth. They are past. They were not really you. They were just an episode. They don't count anymore. They are no longer possible. This, simply and sadly, is often a kind of fundamental denial.

4. **Accepting the disease.** At the core of any illness is acceptance. Not a weak surrender, but a bold and responsible acknowledgement that something about the way your brain or

body works results in harm to you and your functioning way of life. Accepting a mental illness can seem like giving up, or settling, or even flat-out failure. But acceptance is deeply *empowering*. Once you allow that you need to build your life on top of stable conditions, you can learn to play the best cards in your hand in the best possible way. Acceptance is the *beginning*, the precondition for optimizing your present and future.

5. **Live within a zone of stability.** If you were going to climb a mountain, you'd be unwise not to use ropes and to clip in to the metal hardware along the route. After all, you're going out on a limb, risking falls, and taking chances. The climb is life, and it is an exciting but unpredictable state of being. There are falls and setbacks and mistakes and completely human failures. Staying on meds is staying tied into your ropes, so that when you misstep or lose your grip, you are caught and supported rather than plummet to the ground. Meds are what create a zone of safety and stability, so that you can venture outward and climb on.

6. **Then vs. Now.** Once main symptoms are managed, you can develop a false security. In other words, if the symptoms are gone, then you don't need the treatment anymore. While this is sometimes the case for short-term or situational challenges, more serious and deeply ingrained illness doesn't just vanish. It's easy to look at your renewed and improved life and think, "I'm good now, so I'm going to stop taking my meds." But it's often the meds that are the reason you got to where you are, why you are feeling good again, and what are preventing you from backsliding into that place of despair or dysfunction. Meds are a necessary condition of your feeling good now, and removing them would take away the positive effects that feel so entirely present. But the present is a *result* of what you have done to treat your symptoms.

7. **The slippery slope of meds reduction.** In some cases, it's entirely appropriate and healthy to taper down medications under the supervision of a trained clinician. But, there is always a risk of relapse. In some cases you get to "titrate" down your dose and evaluate how you are doing along the way. In other cases, your meds can get low *enough* that you simply lose the insight to honestly judge how you are doing. You can go too far. You can lose control of your ability to keep control. You can spiral downward. It's important to be serious and even skeptical of your own ability to reduce your medications. You are the reporter of how they're working, but your objectivity can disappear as you lower your meds. You need to question if you can remain unbiased even when your plan is not working. And you need a backup system in place if you pass your limits and start to go downhill fast.

8. **Need to pause.** Because lowering meds can be a slippery slope you often need to simply pause—stop in your tracks—and wait. This can be frustrating if you are full of optimism and hope, but it's essential to tracking the return of your *main* symptoms. There is no rush to lower meds. Life is long. Your illness may be with you in some way for years or even decades. Managing and balancing your medications doesn't need to happen on a set timeframe and going too fast is often dangerous or simply unnecessary. If the downside alternative is falling back into your worst self, then *take time* and make sure you're going to *get it right*.

9. **Going back up.** There's a fallacy that if lowering your meds a little worked, that lowering them even more is better. You can get to a point where in your experimental reduction of meds, symptoms are starting to pop back up. And this is where you need to do something seemingly unthinkable: you need to go back *up* on your meds. Recovery sometimes seems like a one-way path to improvement, but it's not. It's an obstacle

course filled with wins and holes. If you are past your point of control, then you need to backtrack so you can keep going forward safely.

10. **Hiding symptoms.** How healed are you? Do you still get passing thoughts of self-harm or moments of despair? Are you occasionally hearing voices or denying yourself healthy options? Recovery doesn't mean the erasure of every instance of your symptoms; often the goal is management, not a 100% cure. When you look at and present your life, are you hiding some of the pieces that run counter to your narrative of self-improvement? If so, before you lower your meds, you should *really* focus on those lingering symptoms. In a way, you have to *earn* the right to come down on meds, and that means doing the work to make sure it will be a positive and safe choice.

11. **Trusting yourself.** A common refrain of all people, and especially those whose lives are disrupted by mental illness, is that they *need to be able to trust themselves*. After all, what is the point of life and recovery if you are hobbled and full of doubt? But trust is a very tricky thing, and it's not an absolute. You can trust yourself in some areas but not in others. For a person with a history of mental illness, you may be entirely trustworthy in your relationships, or your career, or your education, but not in your subjective appraisal of your worst symptoms. They can creep up on you. You can be unaware, or neglectful, or fully in denial about them. This is not a failure of self—it's simply a human reality that we all have blind spots. You can trust yourself, but that means knowing where you need extra help, and where you can't trust yourself alone or fully.

12. **Having a team.** One of the best ways to get a more accurate view of how you're doing is to have not just a doctor but a whole treatment team. In boxing, a fighter will have someone who works on diet, another who focuses on defense, a

third on fitness, a fourth on strength, a fifth on strategy, and a sixth overall manager... you get the idea. Not only does the boxer not fight alone, they rely on a multitude of teachers and trainers and coaches. You can and often need to be like this too. Your treatment team can include your psychiatrist, your therapist, your primary physician, your friends, your parents, even your coworkers. You can take in all of their feedback as valuable data. This doesn't mean you are out of control; it's more like giving up a *little* control in the short term to stay on a long-term path of *maximum* control. Great fighters never fight alone, and you shouldn't either.

13. **Fooling doctors.** This is a tricky one, because trust in doctors is essential to treatment. But doctors can be fooled in two ways. The first way doctors can be fooled is seeing you when you are nice and happy and stable on your medications. Even doctors can fall into the then vs. now trap, because a new doctor may never have seen you at your worst. They didn't see the struggling you, and they *want* to believe that you are capable of change. What they may miss is just how horrible your life was before. The doctor who saw you in the hospital would know you very differently than the new psychiatrist you see once a month after you've stabilized. The second way a doctor can be fooled is if you always present your best self to them. It's natural to want to improve, to please, and to show how much progress you've made. But are you giving a *complete* picture to your doctor? Are you telling them not only how much better you've gotten, but also the symptoms that still linger or have returned? Are you admitting to them how unbearable your life was before treatment? Are you talking to them about the fears and risks of falling back into those patterns? If you only show doctors the upside, they may believe that is the real you, when it's actually only one freshly polished side of the coin.

14. **Consider the risks.** A truck filled with heavy boulders

going up a steep hill doesn't inevitably make it over the top. It needs good traction and a full tank of gas, an alert driver, and a strong engine. If you take out a critical part of the equation, the truck can stall and slide back downhill. It's a hard but mature realization that choices entail the risk that you make the wrong choice. Lowering or stopping medications is a real risk that you need to weigh. You might make it over the top, but what are the odds, and what would you do if you start rolling backwards?

15. **Freedom to choose wrong.** A sense of meaningful control is essential to feeling like life has purpose and possibility. The ability to choose how you manage your mental illness is an important component of your recovery. You *should* feel in control of how you handle this difficult aspect of your life. But being in control and getting to choose comes with immense responsibility to make good choices. Freedom to choose isn't a guarantee that you always choose correctly. Being in control sometimes means knowing your limitations and being in control of when you *stop* lowering medications or even *raise* them. That's real control, and it requires considering all options.

16. **The addiction of avoiding treatment.** This is a hard one to admit, because mental illness is hard enough. It's odd then that someone on meds often feels a strong pull, or even a compulsion, to get off of them. They may miss their *real* self, or the "highs" and "creativity" they felt. They may associate meds with being "trapped" or "controlled". It may feel like the path to freedom and happiness is less meds or no meds. In some cases, the desire to *avoid medications* is as powerful as the temptation an addict feels to *consume drugs*. It can seem like the only thing between you and paradise, or success, or real happiness is getting off your meds. Is that true? Or are you actually motivated by a drive you're not fully aware or in control of? Are you *addicted* to coming off your medication? Are you secretly

skipping doses? Have you tried coming off before only to relapse and wind up back under your covers or in a hospital or out on the street? Are you denying evidence that you *need* meds to be your best possible self?

17. **Imaginary selves.** Any time something external intrudes on our life it's easy to identify it as the source of all of your problems. It's easy to think, "If only I wasn't on these medications I would feel more confident," or "I could get a job if I could just lower my dosage." There may even be a kernel of truth in these mountains of hope, but most often the reality is that the side effects of medications are way outsized in your mind and only slightly relevant to your real wishes. This is a fallacy of causation: you may be unfulfilled and taking meds, but *that does not mean taking meds is the true source of your dissatisfaction*. It could be entirely the opposite: that taking meds is setting you up to even have a chance at getting what you really want.

18. **Tolerating the side effects.** Nothing in this guide is denying that side effects *suck*. They can really cramp your style, dampen your mood, interfere with your plans, and sometimes limit your capabilities. They can make you lethargic, constipated, less able to partake in activities, or just damn chubby. It's not easy being on serious psych meds; that's why so often people abandon the treatment regimen that eased the *main symptoms* of their condition. Side effects are the cost of treating your disease. Your goal and your job is to learn to minimize the side effects and at times just learn to live and move around them. If you gained weight, you may need to adjust your diet or exercise more. If you're tired, you may need to cut back on work responsibilities or take more naps. If you're lacking mental sharpness, it may not be possible for you to tackle the most complex problems. There are sacrifices and compromises to be made along the way. Remember that your

choice is not between more side effects and no side effects. Your choice is between more side effects and more symptoms of your main mental illness.

19. **If it was cancer.** People with mental illness often view themselves, or are viewed by others, as having a fundamentally different *type* of problem—something internal, intrinsic, or personal. In truth, most mental illnesses have a strong neurological and biochemical basis in the brain and nervous system. Consider how you would react if your condition wasn't depression or bipolar disorder but cancer or diabetes. Chemotherapy is awful, but it's generally better than cancer ravaging your body. Cutting out sugary treats is a bummer, but it's a fair deal compared to losing your feet or needing a kidney transplant. Your mental illness is, in addition to a very personal psychological condition, also a medical reality. If you wouldn't skip chemotherapy and insulin injections, you should also hold tight to the medication regimen that is keeping you stable.

20. **Doing it the natural way.** Some people view meds as fundamentally "unnatural". This may come from a preference for holistic, herbal, homeopathic, and alternative medicine or energy healing. It may just be a dislike of pharmaceutical drugs and "chemicals". Nothing against Chinese medicine or Ayurveda or herbs, but the key is that some people just need meds to function and can't replace them solely with alternative therapies. But these can be a great *complement to meds*. Go to acupuncture—and take your meds. Get a cranial-sacral massage—and take your meds. Supplement with Astragalus and Ashwagandha—and take your meds. Treatment is not an either/or proposition. Psych meds aren't demonically different, just like alternative treatments aren't magically successful.

21. **Drug abuse destroys recovery.** Another way to effectively "not take your meds" is to take other drugs that

directly interfere with the way they work. If you are depressed and smoking pot all day, bipolar and doing amphetamines, or anxious and drinking two bottles of wine each night, you are endangering yourself as much as if you just threw out your prescriptions. Psych meds work to balance your brain chemistry and mood, while drugs of "recreation" intentionally unbalance you. Some people can handle this temporarily, but if you're on psych meds you just can't. You're already near the cliff, and it doesn't take much to push you over. It may sound sad that you can't have "fun" anymore, or "take the edge off", but if you're adding drug use or abuse to psych meds you're going to make it impossible to recover.

22. **Remember rock bottom.** Sometimes you have to take a break from your great and inspiring, or brave and incremental recovery. Sometimes you're ascending a ladder into your full potential, and you have to look down. You have to look back at how far you've come, which is the flip side of looking at how far you could fall again. You have to remember the most unbearable, embarrassing, painful parts of your past when you were beyond hopeless or blatantly detached from reality. You have to remember rock bottom. It is harsh to say, but you can hit it again; you could go even deeper next time. Recovery is not guaranteed.

23. **Dead, jailed, homeless, or hospitalized.** This may seem extreme, but for some people it's a simple truth. Going off medications can have dire consequences, including losing your life, winding up in prison, living on the streets, or being involuntarily confined in a mental institution. Your life can be much better, but it can also be much worse. Are your meds, which you love to hate, keeping you from those outcomes? If so, you should accept them even with grudging appreciation.

24. **It's not recovery without resilience.** Let's say your

symptoms are gone for now, out of sight. You're feeling good and behaving better than you can remember in ages. It may seem like that's a good time to cut out those pesky meds. This is a critical time, and it's easy to think you're out of the woods if your recovery is going well. But like that mountain climber who has never fallen before, you don't know if your rope will catch you and hold. Have you been exposed to enough stressors or triggers to know that if you start to wobble you can regain your balance? Have you demonstrated not just recovery from symptoms but *resilience* against those patterns coming back?

25. **Relapse happens, learn from it.** As hard as you try, you might wind up back in the hospital or having episodes again. You could fall into old patterns and lose your job or lash out at friends and family. Despite your sincere efforts, you might misevaluate the severity of your symptoms and be overcome by destructive behavior or detached thinking. Don't give up. You can learn something from each return to the old ways you're trying to grow out of. You can pick up a new lesson each time you "fail". It's not actually failure if you're moving forward with new understanding and awareness of where the pitfalls are.

26. **Focus on the direction not the prescription.** It's easy to become obsessed with one aspect of your existence with mental illness. Too often, that intense focus goes to the thing with a number that comes pressed into a pill you swallow at precise times of the day. Meds are important, sometimes vital, but they are not the story of your life. Rather than think about your value and existence in terms of what drugs you take and how much of them, think about the long arc of your whole journey. It should be filled with friends and laughter and nature and hobbies and passions. Maybe romance, or a career, or children. You could contribute as a volunteer, or make art, or simply take good care of yourself and find pleasure day-to-day. This is what makes up life—not a prescription.

27. **Remember the burden on others.** You're not on this journey alone. While you're the main character in your story—and you own and have to live out your existence—what you choose can have real and often harrowing consequences on those around you. This isn't a guilt trip; it's a reality check. When you lose control from going off meds, other people often pick up the pieces. It could be your girlfriend who has to endure your temper, or your mother who has to visit you in the hospital. It could be your friends who worry where you disappeared to, or your community that suddenly lacks your lovely presence around town. Part of having a team means that people are rooting for you but also hurting with you. Focus on your journey, but keep in mind that you're not a solo actor in this web of life.

28. **It's not fair.** I want to be really, compassionately, lovingly clear: none of this is fair. It's not fair that your brain went haywire, or your emotions are out of your control. It's not fair that you hear things that aren't there or can't stop certain behaviors. It's not fair that you suffered from your symptoms, struggled for months or years because of your condition, or lost friends and jobs along the way. It's not fair that you have to take these drugs that insult, frustrate, constrain, or dull you. It's not fair that you have uncomfortable side effects. It's not fair your doctor or family scrutinizes your behavior. It's not fair that there is social stigma about mental illness. It's all really not fair, and I am totally, completely, genuinely sorry for it. Truth be told, however, none of that has anything to do with the basic choice to stay on or lower your medications. Unfairness is the starting point here; it's not an excuse to make an irresponsible choice.

29. **You're good enough.** I don't know how to say this in a way that will sound convincing, but I will: you're good enough. Even with your underlying illness, or your daily medications,

your imperfect personality, or your sense of failure: *You. Are. Good. Enough.* There is no perfect destination, and wherever you are on the path of recovery, it's really okay to just find peace with it. Sometimes the only way to stay sane is to accept the instability that lies underneath your stability. Sometimes the only way to feel good about yourself is to accept that you're doing the best you can and that's enough. Even with everything you'd love to change or wish were different, there's nothing *wrong* with your life. It's okay as it is, and so are you.

30. **Gratitude**. How can you feel so broken, or have struggled so much, and still be thankful for your life? More than just realizing that "it could be worse", there is a real gift in taking the time to acknowledge, appreciate, and even relish the support you have or the simple joys you've regained. How does it feel to wake up in your own bed and not be wearing a hospital gown? How does it feel to be able to go outside your house and not have it take all of your energy? How does it feel for the voices or thoughts in your head to not distract you from sitting and enjoying a conversation with someone who is genuinely interested in and loves you? These are all moments for simple gratitude, and I promise that gratitude is a gift that gives back to you. It gives hope for even more to be grateful for. It gives peace of mind. And that is no small thing to have.

Hamsa

Go slow my love
In this world
Are a thousand hands
Rubbing your back (as I would do)
Palms pressed against
All your pain
And your heart aching with woes
Go slow my love
Let me catch up with you
So my hands can go home

How to Write a Facebook Suicide Note

1. Be clear: this is the end
2. Offer advice on how to live a good life
3. Give a sense of how you messed up and why you now must die
4. Provide a relevant historical quote
5. Offer inspiration for upcoming events and regrets that you can't participate
6. Tie up loose ends: apologize and offer absolution for all sins
7. State firmly that no one could have helped you
8. Thank those who did try
9. Share gratitude for everyone else you knew
10. Ask people to support your family and acknowledge the pain of your survivors
11. Make one request of those who care about you
12. Ask for forgiveness for the pain your death caused
13. Leave a datestamp of your final birth and end of life years
14. Link to 1-3 YouTube videos that express your love, struggle, and departure
15. Delete the note
16. Call 9-1-1
17. Let experts support you in your crisis
18. Take a medication to reduce your immediate suffering
19. Learn to live with your pain
20. Accept your most critical faults
21. Cry a lot
22. Forgive yourself for everything
23. Face the fear of writing a completely new story for yourself
24. Make a slow but admirable recovery
25. Understand yourself from multiple perspectives
26. Be there for your kids
27. Lean on your friends
28. Understand yourself from multiple perspectives
29. Get a dog

30. Laugh at your own fragility
31. Create a wildly imperfect life
32. Develop a creative form of self-expression
33. Help someone through their hard time
34. Find new love
35. Explore the world together for 50–60 more years
36. Let people share their memories while you can still hear them
37. Look back on your whole journey
38. Say goodbye
39. Rest in peace

For Greg

What Do We Do Now?

Love. Love the people around you. Show them warmth and care and strength and vulnerability today. Show them you are with them. Show them you need them. Show them you will stand up for them and stand beside them.

Resist. Resist the urge to feel crushed or panicked. Resist the temptation to despair. Resist the sense of powerlessness. Resist what threatens love. Resist what threatens nature. Resist what threatens humanity, human decency, human dignity, and human rights.

Connect. Connect to groups that share your fears and won't stop fighting. Connect to your feelings. Connect to your future. Connect to your breath. Connect to music. Connect to your neighbors. Connect to anyone who needs to be affirmed and reassured today. Connect to your creativity, drive, and influence. Connect to your privilege and use the fuck out of it.

Love. Resist. Connect.

How to Save Someone's Life When the only Life You Can Save Is Your Own (Part 4)

Someone's going to break down
Someone's going to come apart
Someone's going to forget what matters
Someone's going to fall
Before you can catch them

And you can run to them
You can give advice
You can gather round friends and family
You can read them poems
But the only life you can save is your own

Someone's going to lose their mind
Someone's going to throw it all away
Someone's going to reject a cure
Someone's going to feel immense pain
That you will not be able to heal

And you can call them up
You can visit them in their hospital gown
You can cry with them on your shoulder
You can even beg
But the only life you can save is your own

Someone's going to hurt themselves
Someone's going to run from their problems
Someone's going to punish the innocent
Someone's going to believe their demons
Even though you're willing to listen

And you can throw them a rope
You can direct them to safety

You can order the right prescription
You can launch an intervention
But the only life you can save is your own

Someone's going to be vicious
Someone's going to self-destruct
Someone's going to slip into despair
Someone's going to spin into crisis
Despite how much you love them

And you can care for them
You can offer them a warm meal
You can hold their hand
You can speak of hope
But the only life you can save is your own

Today, that's enough.
Tomorrow you can see again about saving the world.

Humans of Planet Earth

Sometimes we get a reminder that we are all on a quest for belonging. Sometimes it leaves a mark on us, showing that we are each so deeply human and worthy of love.

On the morning after Donald Trump announced his presidential victory, my Uber driver is from Iraq. I tell him, this is a scary day for America.

No, he says, here I am safe. In Iraq they kidnapped my daughter and make me give money to get her back. So I leave the next day to Jordan. In Jordan they say you can't stay here. Your family is too big. Do you want to go to America, they ask me? And I am here three years now. Under Saddam there was security and food but no money and no life. Now there is no money, and no security. I am refugee.

What about Donald Trump? I ask.

Donald Trump is not good not bad. The one good thing is he is big businessman. So I think he bring more jobs to America. But he also say bad things about Latino, Muslim, Blacks. If they didn't work who would do all the jobs?? I work so I am OK. In America if you work, if you have money you are OK. If not, you have no life here.

...My two sons are born here and they are American. But my two daughters were not born here. My wife and me were not born here. So my sons are American but we are not American. What will Trump do with that???

I ask him if he has met many Jews in Milwaukee.

I don't care about Jew. Or Muslim or Christian. Someone smile at me I smile at them. Someone help me I help them. I tell my children you don't care if Jewish or Muslim or Christian. They are person. They are man, they are woman. If they no believe in my God that is not my business. If they need believe in their God that is their business. That is between God and them.

Welcome to this country, I say to him: You are going to make a great American.

As I am leaving I tell him that my girlfriend speaks Arabic.

You must tell her, he says, *habibi*.

What does it mean, I ask?

It means loved one. All day you say habibi, habibi, habibi.... *my love*.

Goodbye my friend. Good luck.

Sedona

Creekside at night
I swear I could hear the heartbeat of the earth
An intermittent thrum
Deep and sure

Or maybe it was the cars
Passing on the road outside our camp
Shaking the sacred bones beneath the red rocks

Or it was my wife's breath vibrating softly
The closest thing I've found to
A rhythm on this planet

I Am Feeling Lucky Now

On my 34th birthday I wrote down some gratitude…

I want to thank my parents for raising me with an uncompromising love, throwing an infinitude of baseballs and taking me to their favorite beaches, for bouncing me on their knees and playing games of war, and sending me on adventures down canyons, up mountainsides, on preschool playdates, and to college where I learned to learn on my own.

In my life there was a constant group of the most amazing guys. It's a circle that includes Adam—every day after fourth grade I would intentionally miss my bus so I could go over to his house and eat his cereal and play tennis and his video games. He taught me how to laugh, and how to know just what you could say to someone before they would think you took it too far. His method, of course, was taking it just too far, from which I deduced precisely where too far was, and then could go just barely up to it.

It includes David from summer camp who had a hammer of loyalty that he would occasionally whack me with if I was getting off track, an incredible frisbee toss, and an eye for noticing beauty around him—and if others couldn't see it he would make sure, forcefully if necessary, that they did.

I'd like to thank Kumar for teaching me that genius is not intelligence, but drive welded to curiosity—for example, drive to finish a video game and curiosity to wonder what an Xbox controller coated in Subway red onions feels like after you hand it over to your freshman roommate for a turn.

I'd like to thank Matt for showing me that life is not tragedy; it's poker. You stay in the game, and when you have the edge put all your chips in. Win big in the long run. It's amazing to see you already parenting two kids. Slow down man, manage your stack!

I'd like to thank Drucker, for being so freaking handsome, for not hitting on any women in my life, and for bringing your intense love of making art come alive into the world, contagiously, seductively... but I digress.

I'd like to thank Sippy for trusting that pretentious poetry is really just a young mind trying to form a world around it. And for trying to save that world with even more eloquent words.

I'd like to thank Aaron. First, for being a good listener and a psycho-logical ninja. Second, you have done things embarrassing enough that I don't have to feel shame anymore. Third, you have been an incomparable friend. *Ceteris paribus*, I wouldn't have chosen anyone else to live across from me or walk me back into the world.

The boys are the most uncouth gods that Zeus ever dropped from heaven to come and revive a man dying under blankets with a riveting game of Settlers of Catan.

I want to thank my sisters, for going on journeys that brought back lessons I would have been too timid to learn on my own. For Ray, who motivated me every day of my youth to push myself, mostly so that I could best her in Gotcha Last, and later to think more deeply about what surrounded me. And recently to not forget too much, while we move on with our futures. To Bec, for not wanting to play baseball and charting her own unique, meticulous, and ambitious course. You have shown that having a dream in life pays off if you are willing to work and sacrifice for it. To both my sisters, I owe thousands of conversations and bursts of hilarity across the dining room table.

I'd like to thank my grandmothers, the soft chubby one, and then also bubby, for giving me without reservation all of their delightful personality and hugs and humor.

I'd like to thank my aunts and uncles (and cousins!), real and adopted, for each giving me a piece of myself that I didn't know I had. You remind me that we are broader than one variation on a genome, wiser, wackier, more inquisitive, more patient.

I'd like to thank my Wikipedia friends, too numerous and globally distributed to number. You have been fine companions in our crazy quest to create a community that can share knowledge with the world. At its best, that is a sacred calling, and you are incredible allies and good company on that mission we take on together.

I was a model child, nary a rebellious or rude moment, up and through my teens. I'd like to thank my parents for enduring the rich payback of my 20s where I did everything in my power to upend those roots. Thank you for making sure I stopped digging before I proved I could.

I'd like to thank my high school wrestling coach Jim, who after an unexpected loss, told me that I was playing it too close to the vest. He meant on the wrestling mat, but it had implications without boundaries in my future.

I'd like to thank Chip for making sure I took the walk, and the flight, and never treating me like I couldn't handle it.

I'd like to thank that gentle psychiatrist who sat with me and listened for days about all of the obstacles I was clinging to. And then after a long pause said, "You know, it's not too late to have everything you want... but one day it will be." I look around today and I know exactly what he meant.

I want to thank the choice I made to hop on a bus to Washington DC in 2012 where I had to meet Siko, who I was sure was French Polynesian, so that I could find someone to have faith in me and my vision. That $20 bus ticket turned out to be worth an uncountable fortune.

It was months after I got back from that DC conference when my dad stopped asking who I was chatting with, because he already knew by the sheer look on my face—eyes shining, cheeks glowing, lips spread wide across my face with held-in laughter. I couldn't conceal it, it just erupted through me. He dubbed it my Siko Face.

We went out for dumplings in Hong Kong, bratwurst in Germany, curries in London, tacos in Mexico City, cocktails in San Francisco, and ceviche in San Diego.

When you invited me to California for the first time, you opened the door—literally, you had just picked up Z, and warned me before bringing her home that she might not be so warm at first. The door ajar, that three-year-old stared and shouted, "Jake!!!" and started running into my arms sooner than I could get down on my knees to hug her back. Thank you for letting me in.

I'd like to thank Z for inviting me to play with her in the morning while others are sleeping, and for being an excellent breakfast bread co-chef, for taking me on walks to pick flowers and other people's fruit, for showing me the *right* way to throw a frisbee, and for letting me come back from trips with bags of presents that are Definitely Not For Her. For being creative, silly, strong, smart, and fearless. For proving to me that girls can wrestle, and like her mom, showing me that wrestling with girls who are fierce radical modern competitors can be as thrilling as it is dangerous for many parts of my body.

I'd like to thank Siko's family, for welcoming me from day one—with teases and tips only a big brother could offer, gluten-free apricot almond cookies and rooms surrounded by colorful and enchanting art, spirit card readings, hand-crafted chocolate truffles, gratis lessons in freedom of body movement, a place to crash in San Francisco and walks around Seattle, hikes up the Hollywood hills and paper dresses, farm-to-table graduation brunches, escapes into high mountains, and no less, the chance to be an uncle to four wily boys before I even realized that was possible for me. To my three new sisters, two new brothers, four new moms, two new dads, two aunts and one uncle, four nephews, and even the mule-biting cousin John... Thanks for treating me so well. And to Anna, Lon, Nancy, Ilana, Linda, Burt... thank you for being there, for sharing your homes and hearts, talents and wisdom, with my girl.

I'd like to thank Lucas and Melanie for being trustworthy co-parents. I feel very, very good going to sleep at night knowing that Z has—at least—four incredibly engaged, thoughtful people looking out and up for her each day.

But for the best, I'd like to thank Siko. For finding my confessional and nervous approach to our first conversations endearing. For showing me there was more to life than even Wikipedia! For being the best menu-ordering partner I have encountered in my entire life. I, renowned for my culinary picks, have never misordered a single dish with you. Together we can eat the ideal meal in any restaurant setting anywhere on the planet, and if that is not a metaphor for What This Is, then I give up the search for a better comparison.

I'd like to thank you for growing with me. For re-teaching me how to snuggle. For helping me learn how to be teased. For taking me on adventure after adventure. Thank you for helping me be hard when life demands it. Thank you for practicing being soft when we depend on it to grow. Thank you for saying "OK... Yes", when I asked if you wanted to get married.

You taught me, in your wise and persevering ways, that family comes in a million different shapes and colors, and life is all the more interesting and wonderful for it. I never would have imagined that family looks like me, you and Z, sitting on paddle boards wearing wetsuits a mile out from the beach watching a sea otter cuddle its baby on a patch of 40-foot-tall seaweed in the marine sanctuary of our backyard. I have learned to trust that whatever my preconception, you have often imagined it better than I.

I am proud of your initiative, boldness, creativity, perception, loyalty, and love. With you I'm often enamored, frequently challenged, never bored, and ever evolving. In the mornings I wake up from sweaty dreams and wrap myself around you in the best five minutes of my day. At nights you take my arm before you bury your head and use it like a thermopedic pillow with a death grip on my bicep. I hope you never let it go.

To all the people in my life and whom I've met along my journey, thank you.

Hafiz Remixed on the Eve of My Wedding

Daniel Ladinsky's translations, in a new shape...

the stars got poured out of a magician's hat last night
the million candles are lit and singing
every particle of existence is a dancing altar
we live on the sun's playground
with each sublime whirl and orbit

when the moon is full
it gets gregarious and likes to chat
i have heard it say

the sky is a suspended blue ocean
the stars are the fish that swim
tie yourself to spawning stars
and to leaping whales

tie your soul like a magnificent sweet chime
to every leaf and limb
grab hold and swing from me

let's turn loose our golden falcons
so that they can meet in the sky
where our spirits belong

we are a spinning wheel upon the infinite
in a game of tag with the moon

we should lean against each other
our hearts should do this more

we are partners
straddling the universe
come dance with me

For Those Seeking Support

The bravest thing to do is ask for help...

This book may have brought up a lot of feelings for you. It may have helped you confront old wounds, or grapple with present crises. You may be thinking of a loved one in despair or danger. I encourage you to reach out and use as many tools as possible to seek safety and to make recovery possible. No one grows alone. Find your helpers.

The following resources are based in the U.S. There are similar organizations in many parts of the world.

- In emergencies, dial 9-1-1. Tell them it's a mental health situation.

- Anytime you need, call the Suicide Prevention Lifeline: 1-800-273-8255

- Find local treatment with the SAMHSA Referral Helpline: 1-877-726-4727

- Get support as a friend or family member through NAMI: 1-800-950-6264

Stories and reading are powerful tools. I especially like graphic novels for reducing the fear of confronting and understanding illness. Here are some favorites:

- *Lighter Than My Shadow*, by Katie Green
- *It's All Absolutely Fine: Life Is Complicated So I've Drawn It Instead*, by Ruby Elliot
- *The Worrier's Guide to Life*, by Gemma Correll
- *Fun Home: A Family Tragicomic*, by Alison Bechdel

- *Bitter Medicine: A Graphic Memoir of Mental Illness*, by Olivier Martini and Clem Martini
- *Hyperbole and a Half: Unfortunate Situations, Flawed Coping Mechanisms, Mayhem, and Other Things That Happened*, by Allie Brosh
- *Marbles: Mania, Depression, Michelangelo, and Me: A Graphic Memoir*, by Ellen Forney
- *Just Peachy: Comics About Depression, Anxiety, Love, and Finding the Humor in Being Sad*, by Holly Chisholm

If you're interested in treatment but not quite ready to do it with another person, try out some of the many credible self-help workbooks. Those that employ Cognitive Behavioral Therapy (CBT) or Dialectical Behavioral Therapy (DBT) are especially well-supported by psychologists and scientific studies.

Lastly, talk to someone. It can be anyone you trust enough to say, "I'm having some trouble," or, "It's been hard for me lately." You can get a great deal of relief just from sharing what's on your mind. This is a simple way to unburden yourself and find tools and next steps.

It's brave to seek out help. It makes your life better. It helps you grow and deal with life's challenges. Try it. You'll be glad you did.

Parting Thoughts

My mission with this book is to impact each person who has personally experienced or witnessed the struggle of mental illness. To end the stigma and shame that prevents people from getting the help they need. To show that recovery is possible, that mental illness can be survived, and that harrowing experiences can be transformed into a dynamic and thriving new chapter of life.

My goal is to make a positive change in people's journeys, to shift society towards compassion and acceptance, and to move each of us towards a fuller realization of our precious and vibrant potential.

You can help share this message with the world, so that you can grow, and so that you can better understand and help others along your path.

I leave with a favor to ask. If you think someone could use help, offer to read a piece with them, or print a copy of an article and ask if it's okay to share it with them. Sit down with someone you love and just ask them how they are doing. Then, with openness and sincerity, just listen. In your own moments, when it feels safe, reflect on where you have suffered, struggled or felt pain. Show yourself kindness and gratitude for where you have been and what you have become. Know that you're not alone, and that you will always be learning and evolving.

This journey doesn't have an endpoint. It's a conversation that spans a lifetime, and even generations. To heal, and to grow, we need to pull up our chairs, sit down, speak our own stories, and listen to those around us. In other words, *now that you're part of the circle, invite others to join you.*

Acknowledgements

I've thanked many people, in the dedication of this book, and in the pieces themselves. In fact, one whole piece is just a giant *thank you!* But if there's one thing I've learned, it's that you cannot have too much gratitude. So, I want to recognize and appreciate some of the special helpers and heroes I've had the joy of meeting along my way.

I need to thank my parents again, who showed me immense love as a child, and then suffered confusion and despair when I disappeared for nearly a decade. They didn't know it, but that too was part of my healing, and looking back I can only show my gratitude that they never stopped trying or loving. Ultimately, they put me back on the path to recovery.

I need to thank my sisters. Their journeys had their own bumps and obstacles, but they helped me learn about new tools and higher forms of dedication and grace. As a family, each of us has taught the others from our mistakes, and we have become more bonded from the struggles, not less.

I need to thank my inescapable friends, who not only stood by me in the hardest times, but made them almost intolerably fun. When I nearly wanted to suffer the most, when I resisted life most ferociously, I couldn't help but laugh at their constant and absurd humour and zest for life.

I need to thank my wife, for being not only a rock, but a mountain. You've given me perspective and purpose and the best company a person could seek in a partner. Every day with you I continue to grow, and I appreciate everything you have brought into my life.

I need to thank the quirky and genius community of Wikipedians, who accepted me into their fold without knowing anything about my faults or missteps. You gave me the chance to rediscover my intellect and my voice. You are more than a website, you are a movement shaping the world towards openness and knowledge. You gave me a calling, and I will always be grateful for that.

I need to thank my therapists, doctors, and psychiatrists. I can't name all of them, but each one gave me a piece of the puzzle to put myself back together and to build whole new parts.

I need to thank my early readers, who gave me invaluable feedback and encouragement. Kathy, Jessamyn, Sippy, Siko, Linda, Krishna, Ray, and Emma... you helped me dig deeper, write more, organize better, and shape something I am truly proud of. I could not have done it without your time, attention, energy, love, and wisdom. And Nikki, your incomparable copy editing made the final difference.

Lastly, I need to thank you, the reader. You took a chance on me. And in some ways you took a chance on yourself, to learn about parts of life that are often in the shadows of the world or inside of us. That's brave. That gives me hope. I wish you continued peace and healing wherever you are on this planet, wherever you are on your journey.

-Jake Orlowitz

About the Author

Jake Orlowitz is a seeker of well people and sane societies, an internet citizen, a digital project manager, and an ally and activist for radical culture change. For the last half-decade he has written about mental health and recovery on Medium.com in the *J Curve* publication.

Jake founded and ran The Wikipedia Library program, and built *The Wikipedia Adventure* learning game. He is a native of Main Line Philadelphia and a graduate of Wesleyan University's College of Social Studies.

Jake lives in Santa Cruz, California with his intrepid wife and stepdaughter. They like to walk along the cliffs of the Monterey Bay while drinking agua fresca, looking for dolphins and sea otters swimming in the tall kelp. Recovered from a decade of illness that sent him into a mental hospital, Jake is very lucky and very grateful to be able to help others on their journey.

Reach out any time: jorlowitz@gmail.com or [@JakeOrlowitz](https://twitter.com/JakeOrlowitz). He'd love to hear from you.

Made in the USA
San Bernardino, CA
09 February 2020